Let Not Your Heart Be Troubled

The Universe is Friendly

by John Schroeder

ISBN: 978-0-9843059-8-8

Printed in the U.S.

Table of Contents

Dedication and Thanks

Many have helped me along my spiritual path. The two greatest earthly sources of spiritual information in my life have been my mother, Helen Ruth Schroeder, and Edgar Cayce's psychic readings. My mother's inspiring journey, from being born in dire poverty during the Great Depression to accepting God as her unconditionally loving Father, is a book in itself. The Edgar Cayce readings have also given me a loving perspective of our Father that has made all the difference in my life.

My wife, Stephanie, has also been a patient inspiration for me. No one has helped me write this book more than she, not only in her loving application of all that Jesus taught us but also in reading and editing every word and letting me know when my inspired prose was too "out of this world" to make sense of it on earth.

There were many others who offered their feedback to me one chapter at a time. For those of you who saw how this started, you know what an impact you had after seeing this book completed. My sincere thanks to all of you for taking the time and caring enough to help me clarify these concepts. I would be remiss if I didn't thank Mary Travis for all her help in editing. Mary went through every word, finding typos the rest of us had missed. She even suggested the final title for the book. What a blessing she has been!

Most of all, I dedicate this book to the Holy Spirit, who never leaves us. Only our loving Father could understand how to connect with and draw the best out of me so that I could share it with others. God knows I certainly didn't start as a competent writer. That journey alone was worth the effort. If others find hope and encouragement in the words written here, you also know that we have nothing to fear in this friendly universe.

Introduction

What would we ask if we could ask just one question of God? Ironically, the best response to all my queries doesn't mention God at all: "Is the universe friendly?" I first heard this posed by my mother when I was around 9 years old. She attributed it to Albert Einstein, but I've since found earlier versions of this question quoted from other great minds. Regardless of who said it, the importance of the answer remains with me to this day.

Have you already answered the question for yourself? Perhaps you are still considering what "friendly" means to you and the implications that a yes or no answer might provide. Were you comforted, intrigued, or perhaps frightened by the question and the consequences of the answer? Most importantly, which of those responses indicates we're on the right track?

The Bible says that fear of the Lord is the beginning of wisdom. Logically speaking, if wisdom is based on fearing God, the universe may be unfriendly. I couldn't take this verse at face value because it felt wrong. It is my experience that the interpretations of many Bible verses change according to our optimistic or pessimistic view of life. Fearing God is a good example.

For instance, I have personally found fear to be discouraging rather than motivating in the long run. My greater successes in life have come from feeling good about myself, others, and especially about my relationship with God. On the other hand, some people think fear helps us avoid sin and displeasing God. Those opposing perspectives can often predict our answer to the question, "Is the universe friendly?"

My answer is an emphatic yes—it is friendly. Fear, guilt, and shame can discourage us from wrongdoing, but I see using such methods as resorting to "plan B" rather than thriving in harmony with God and His friendly universe.

I see "plan A" (the universe is friendly) as the preferred perspective for an optimist and "plan B" (the universe is unfriendly) working better for a pessimist. While we can improve ourselves with either plan, I feel it is a lesser choice to believe we live in an unfriendly universe. Choosing plan A or plan B is often, in my opinion, a question of how successfully we communicate with God.

If we believe God won't take the time to talk with us, then our relationship with Him is fragile at best. If we believe there are conditions behind God's love for us, then disobeying Him puts the entire universe against us. If everyone falls short of His perfection, can we ever imagine ourselves in His presence without feeling doubt, fear, or guilt?

Believing the universe is friendly and that our Father loves each of us unconditionally supports our better relationship with Him. If we expect love, encouragement, and great advice every time we open our hearts and minds to God, what a difference that makes in our lives. We find ourselves actively seeking His help no matter what we have done rather than trying to hide, as Adam did, from an unfriendly God.

This book is based on two fundamental premises: that our Father and His universe are indeed friendly and that we can directly receive His perfect, loving answers to our questions. I have been asking questions of God for many years using what is often called inspirational writing. Unlike some "spirit plane communication methods," where others are invited to take control of the body, inspirational writing uses prayer and meditation to help us turn within to the Holy Spirit, where God's kingdom truly resides.

The chapters of this book offer edited transcriptions of the questions I posed and the answers I received through inspirational writing. I believe the Holy Spirit is the source of these answers, and this information is available to everyone who patiently asks and listens with a loving intent. However, the answers we receive will not be the same for any two people. This is because we can't help but filter information according to our preconceptions and experiences. My bias is that the universe is friendly, God is unconditional love, and because He desires to save us all, no soul is ever lost despite our free will.

If you are open to believing God and His universe are loving and friendly, I invite you to explore our relationship with our Father and each other, as the Holy Spirit has revealed to me.

Parting Words from the Start

Q: These chapters have reached a natural conclusion, and it's time to end this book.

A: You have indeed covered a lot of subjects. To be sure, what we share now would make a better first chapter despite being the last written chronologically.

Q: That makes sense in giving the reader a feel for the flow of the Q&A format used throughout the book. I'm glad this is finally ready. It was challenging to know when to say, "This is enough."

A: It is good that you persevered to get to this point. So many start with the best intentions and do not complete their goal.

Q: I'm not sure I can say what goal I had in mind in writing this book. Perhaps it is best described as a primer for living on the earth. Everyone seems to have unique perspectives on life, and mine, as recorded here, is just one more. Is there worthwhile or lasting value in offering one more spiritual perspective among many?

A: More than you know. Many who will read your words have not yet decided what they believe. You offer them a joyful and loving perspective that can enrich their lives if they choose to accept such.

Q: Is all that I have recorded here the truth? I would not want to suggest or offer anything that is not accurate.

A: If offering God's strictly inerrant and infallible words were the criteria for publishing any book, even the Bible would not have made it to print. No matter what is written, it is always subject to the author's free will and the reader's choice to accept or reject what they find helpful and hopeful. The truth is there and available as recorded from your perspective. Our Father asks no more of us than that. As we use what He has given, more will be added.

Q: It seems this book contains one or more concepts that disagree with each "beta test" reader. I don't know how to feel about that.

A: Considering the subjects you took on, what did you expect? What you included in this book is consistent with the unconditionally loving ways of our Father. You can be content with what you have written. Of course, others may disagree with you so much that they are motivated to record their perspectives to clarify the truth as they see it. This would be an excellent outcome for anyone who reads these words. You have learned much and clarified your understanding by going through this process.

Q: One of the objections to this book is the use of a male gender when referring to God. I could just as easily refer to God as a female since I don't believe God has a gender, but I find it awkward trying to describe a personal relationship with God that is less than "parental." I go with the male gender because that was what Jesus used. Why do you most often refer to God using the male gender?

A: Because that is your preference. If you preferred to think of the "I am that I am" as Creator, Loving Spirit, First Cause, Father/Mother/God, or any of the other terms that are gender neutral, I would be using those instead. Regardless, it should be clear to all that our Creator has no gender or gender bias.

Q: Another objection is that I have not identified a specific person as the source for this book. Who am I talking to in the responses I receive?

A: The only "source" for anything is our Father. Nothing exists without Him. He is the perfect ideal for all creation. As His free-willed children, we can make choices He wouldn't, but the knowledge, power, and ability to do anything always start with Him.

Q: But it feels like my own thinking when I write inspirationally. Why is that?

A: You say that as if you have nothing to offer of yourself. Why were we created? We were intended to be co-creators and companions with Him. To constantly sit on the sidelines admiring everything others have done instead of becoming personally involved is giving up our gift of free will. Learning to make choices where everyone wins while still being in harmony with our Father's loving ways becomes easier with practice. When we ask for guidance with this intention, it should feel like our thoughts come from the Holy Spirit within.

Q: But what about when Jesus said, "I only do what I see the Father doing"? Doesn't that imply we are not to interfere with God's will?

A: To hinder perfection is neither satisfying nor successful in the long run. However, your statement implies there is only one perfectly loving choice in any situation. As co-creators, our purpose is to make choices that bring us the greatest joy while still being in accord with the Holy Spirit, also known as the law of love. There are often many loving choices available where everyone wins, but it is up to us to decide which will make us and everyone else the happiest.

Q: Are you saying there are no absolutes regarding what is right and wrong?

A: The only "sin" is selfishness, meaning that whatever we do from a loving intent does no harm from a spiritual or lasting perspective. "Right and wrong," as you called them, are best discerned through our thoughts and intentions rather than our actions alone. We can and do make choices that are not in harmony with God's loving ways, but our good efforts are still counted for righteousness.

Q: That reminds me of the parable of the Pharisee and the Tax Collector, where they were both outwardly praying, but the Pharisee was doing so from ego. The Tax Collector was contrite in his prayers, knowing he was far from perfect yet wanting to improve. Is that the idea?

A: Yes. It doesn't matter what we are doing or why we are doing it. Thinking we are better than others does not help us to become better people. It is important to note that feeling worse than others does not help us improve.

Q: As is pointed out often in these chapters, achieving balance in all things is an important goal. A goal I had in writing this was to achieve a balance between putting too much and too little information into each chapter. How did I do?

A: You know this already. You did not err by putting in too much, and what you did offer will serve to whet the appetites of those who see life as you do. Each chapter included here could and eventually will be the catalyst for other books.

Q: As I often ask at the end of each chapter, what words of encouragement can you offer as I officially close and technically begin the book with this final chapter?

A: Your strengths have always included perseverance and inertia. Many could learn from this, for remaining in motion allows for greater progress than standing still. That is not to say that "you can do no wrong," but because you most often make choices with the highest intent, the universe literally rearranges itself to support you. Continue to move forward without fear or regret, and always see how to make loving choices so that everyone wins. In so doing, you cannot ultimately fail.

My Own Healing Experience

When I was perhaps nine or ten years old, I came down with a very high fever and an awful sore throat. This was typical of my childhood illness pattern, and I knew that I would probably not be well again for three or four days. I was lying in bed asleep that first night when my mother came in and woke me. I was annoyed since sleep was the one time I had some relief from the pain.

She ushered a man into the room who was a gifted healer. He was a member of the Edgar Cayce spiritual study group meeting in our house weekly. After hearing I was ill, he offered his help by "laying on of hands."

I was told to lie still while he held his hands above my throat area for a few minutes. I was still groggy and did as they asked, although I vaguely wondered what was happening. I began to feel an unusual warmth in my throat, which got my attention. I continued to monitor my body for other sensations, but my throat seemed to be the focus of the warmth.

After about 10 minutes of this, I needed to swallow. Because my throat had been so sore, I would try to swallow as little as possible. When I finally did, I braced myself for the pain that I knew was coming. When I felt no pain at all, I swallowed again and then again. I said aloud, "It doesn't hurt anymore."

Looking back on this event, I realize it was a key moment because of their reaction to my healing. Both my mother and the man, John Miley, said the same thing almost together, "Well, of course it doesn't." Their response served to cement in my mind an essential foundation by which the universe operates. It confirmed that faith in the healing power of love is a natural thing that should not surprise us. We should expect it every time we ask for God's help with a loving attitude and purpose. I doubt I would have learned that lesson at such a deep level had either my mother or John Miley shown any surprise at the "miracle" that had just occurred.

The Nature of God

Q: When I read the Bible, which is said to be the infallible word of God, I read many conflicting accounts regarding what God is like. Do all the accounts in the Bible describe the true nature of God?

A: No, but this is always subject to each soul's perspective. All Biblical descriptions of God reflect the author's understanding of our relationship with our Creator, but not necessarily the truth of our Father's loving nature.

Q: Your answer would imply that much of the Bible is false, especially in the Old Testament. Is that what you're saying?

A: No. Here is a better way to see this. If you ask a question in English and get an answer in French, did you receive the wrong answer, or were your expectations not met in the kind of answer you received? The answers we seek can be found in the Bible, although they are given outside of the expectations most people have because of what they already believe.

Q: Let's try something specific. The Bible says He is a jealous God. Is that true?

A: No. The Bible verses that say such reflect a lack of faith in our Father's unconditional love and omniscience. The message conveyed to the Biblical authors was that there is only one loving Creator, and it is in Him that we live, move, and have our very being. Why bother searching further for another answer when there is none?

When seen through the eyes of fear and a lack of trust, such a loving concept would see this invaluable advice as coming from a jealous God. The suggestion that we love our Father as the First Cause and Creator of all is accurate. That we should do so because He is a jealous God is a human invention. A better interpretation is still available for all to see despite the "human version" of the truth. Our karmic suffering on Earth causes many to believe in a lesser God. The resulting void created by their unbelief in His unconditional love is then filled with fear and mistrust.

Q: But the Biblical authors are believed to have transcribed the Word of God directly as if by dictation. Is that not true?

A: When it was written that He is a jealous God, that was as loving a description as the Biblical authors could interpret from the truth that was given. If you consider the entire Bible a historical perspective of our growing understanding of our Father's unconditional love, it makes much more sense and is easier to interpret.

Q: So God did not instruct Moses to kill, rape, and pillage the non-believers, as the Bible tells us?

A: Of course not. But when coming from a place of fear, guilt, and shame, it is not so difficult to understand why Moses felt he was guided to do such things.

Q: What did God say to Moses that he misconstrued as "orders" to act violently against others?

A: Our Father does not "order" violence, ever. What is often misunderstood by humans is that our spiritual progress is best measured in how patiently we respond to others. When our Father suggested to Moses that the Promised Land ultimately belongs to His people, how might Moses have interpreted such words? A patient person who does not see violence or coercion as an option would see gentle alternatives that Moses did not. When we put time limits on our choices because of our impatience to achieve a goal, it is easy to see how loving options are ignored.

Q: It sounds like you're saying that it was the Jews' shared impatience to possess the Promised Land that made violence appear to be their best choice when it was not. That raises the question, "Do the ends ever justify the means?"

A: Simply said, no. Taking a wrong action to accomplish any amount of good is not in accord with the will of our Father. What can be deceiving is that all things still work to good for those who love Him. So, while violence is not the better answer, the unconditional love of God will ultimately prevail. Some would believe a seemingly positive outcome that started with violence might justify it. This is not true, though our perspective of available choices can become so narrow that we cannot see any other way.

Q: So you have said God is not jealous, impatient, or violent. You did say that God is unconditionally loving. The Bible also tells us that vengeance is His. What exactly does that mean as opposed to what is commonly believed or expected?

A: There is vengeance, and then there is the law of karma. The difference between them is the attitude and intention behind each. Karma is simply a lawful and instructive reaping of what we've sown. It happens naturally, and our Father does not rejoice in the suffering we may endure. Vengeance is "karma with attitude," to put it in today's language. It is one thing to be the neutral channel through which others reap what they sow. It is quite another for us to take pleasure in causing the suffering of others regardless of how "deserving" we feel they might be.

Q: So when the Bible states that vengeance is His, what is the true meaning of that concept?

A: Since it would be tough for humans to choose to be a channel for others to reap what they have sown and still be unconditionally loving toward them, it is better to leave such things to our Father. He will never rejoice when we suffer. Instead, He created the law of karma to learn a better way to live and avoid further suffering with each new opportunity and choice.

Q: And what of the verses in the Bible where it says God hated? Is there any truth to that?

A: None. Never.

Q: But it was written in the Bible that God loved Jacob and hated Esau. That is often interpreted to mean that Jacob's descendants are God's chosen people and the descendants of Esau are not. Was that perhaps speaking of them as individuals? Maybe it was talking about their conflicting spiritual beliefs?

A: Our Father does not hate...period. Love is the only source of power in existence. While free will allows us to choose against His loving ways, hate can only exist when we selfishly misuse His power. Hate, unlike love, has a beginning, so every hateful choice we make will ultimately have an end. Nothing but love is eternal.

Q: The Bible says there is such a thing as "the unpardonable sin." Is there any truth to that?

A: To answer your question, blasphemy against the Holy Spirit is not an unpardonable sin, or almost everyone on Earth would be doomed. From our Father's perspective, no sin is unforgivable. We can choose not to forgive ourselves or others for any sin at any time.

Q: Are some sins worse than others as God sees them?

A: The only worthy measurement of our sinful choices is how difficult it is to get back on track after choosing such. Any sinful behavior we become addicted to is often the toughest to overcome.

Q: I understand that the Bible's descriptions of God as jealous, hateful, and vengeful came from the Old Testament when our understanding of unconditional love was all but non-existent. But the unpardonable sin was written in Matthew and Mark from the New Testament. How could that have been an improvement in our growing understanding of God?

A: That was not an improvement, but it does show how difficult it is to let go of things we have believed for so long. When we blaspheme against the Holy Spirit, as the Bible warns not to, we are blaspheming against the law of love.

To put this into perspective, the teachings of Jesus were relatively new to the world. Many people had wrongly believed in a jealous, vengeful, and even hateful God. Jesus made it clear that our Father and the Holy Spirit are love. The Biblical authors, unwilling to let go of their fear, chose blasphemy against the Holy Spirit (love) as the new "unpardonable sin" to replace the erroneous belief that our Father is hateful, jealous, and vengeful. This was a step in a better direction, but we do indeed learn slowly.

Q: It seems ironic to accept that love is the very foundation of patience, mercy, and forgiveness while believing that blasphemy against love is the one thing that can irreversibly condemn us. That makes no sense.

A: The same could be said of any belief we hold that is not in accord with the will of our Father. It is much easier to explain the truth than it is to make sense of our selfish choices.

Q: I've approached this topic by starting with verses in the Bible instead of first asking you to lay the foundation. Better late than never, I suppose. How would you describe the true nature of God?

A: There is nothing to fear from our loving Father. There is no downside in Him. When truly communing with our Creator, we will experience unconditional love, encouragement, hope, mercy, patience, support, guidance, and fellowship. Our Father is our constant companion, best friend, and perfect counselor because He knows us better than we know ourselves. He desires that we come to know Him equally as well. When we are at our absolute best, it is easy to see that we are indeed made in His perfect image. No matter what we do, our Father never stops loving us.

Q: I really should have started with that question. I guess it shows that getting caught up in a topic's "human perspective" can hinder us from discerning the truth. I've noticed that you most often refer to God as our Father. Is that on purpose?

A: Absolutely. For He is God to all, but He is Father to those who seek His loving ways as their own. Our Father is not a person as we typically think of such, but we can have as close a relationship with Him as we desire. Who could we be closer to any soul except He, who created us in His perfect image?

Q: When do you refer to Him as God rather than Father?

A: Looking back on this discussion will offer much of the answer. When discussing jealousy, hate, and vengeance in connection to our Creator, I used the word God. Also, saying God is appropriate if I speak strictly of a lawful or "cause and effect" relationship. However, He is better described as our Father when we seek His loving ways for our own. Each soul decides what their relationship with Him will be.

Q: And why do you often refer to God using male pronouns?

A: Because that is your preference. If you preferred to think of the "I am that I am" as Creator, Loving Spirit, First Cause, Father/Mother/God, or any of the other terms that are gender neutral, I would be using those instead. Regardless, it should be clear to all that our Creator has no gender or gender bias.

Q: The Bible also quotes Jesus as using male pronouns when referring to God. Was that accurate?

A: Yes, and for the same reasons. For instance, if Jesus publicly referred to God as our Mother, it would have been far too confusing to the people of that time. It was difficult enough to help change the idea that our Father was jealous, vengeful, and hated most of His children. However, if the question was asked about God having a gender, Jesus always made it clear that was not an issue.

Q: I "hear" what you offer as if you were another person. Who am I "speaking" to when I pray for the highest guidance for the answers I seek?

A: As you have asked, it has been given unto you. Whether you assign a name to the "I am that I am" or not makes little difference. The answers you receive will be the same whether they come from Jesus, the Holy Spirit, or any other name you prefer. The more loving you become, the greater the Truth will shine through in what you receive and record.

Q: But you speak as if you were also entrapped here on Earth with the rest of us going through the same trials and lessons as those who have made selfish choices. Why is that?

A: We are in this life together. I am always with you regardless of where you go and what you experience. I am not just an observer of what happens to you. We are One! I have an eternal and parental stake in seeing that you and every other soul become all you were created to be. Whether you make your bed in heaven or hell, I provide a way of escape whenever needed.

Q: You bring to mind the ongoing question of the existence of an eternal hell or even the destruction of the soul. With all that you've said, I'll assume both are false beliefs. What is a compelling reason why such "judgments" are not in God's nature?

A: That question is getting a little ahead of the foundation needed for the answer.

Once we accept that our Father is all-knowing and all-powerful, we will eventually understand that our Father is unconditionally loving. One of the greatest truths in the Bible is that our Father is unwilling to lose any soul. Another is that with every temptation, our Father has already provided a way of escape. Those truths together are the basis for the salvation of us all.

Q: With that in mind, "What is a compelling reason why such things as an irreversible hell or destroying the soul are not in God's nature?"

A: If our Father is unwilling to lose any soul and has the desire and ability to save us all despite our free will, then why wouldn't He?

Q: I have offered a similar perspective in discussions with others. Traditional Christians respond that just because I would prefer it be that way (that we're all saved) doesn't make it so. What should I have said differently?

A: Nothing you could say would change the opinions of those who believe, as you just said. The idea that there is no downside to our Father is not popular with many people. The concept that "there must be losers for there to be winners" is often reinforced in our daily lives. Such a limited or earthly perspective supports the belief that not every soul is worthy of our Father's love.

Q: But isn't it blasphemy against the Holy Spirit to believe that God would condemn or destroy His children? It seems a God of unconditional love with all knowledge and power would have devised a better plan. How did religions end up believing God can't save us all?

A: Because we are still searching for the correct answers. Parts of the traditional Christian creed are the result of a lack of faith in our Father, a lack of trust in our neighbors, and low self-esteem. Yet, religion serves a great purpose in helping to bring people back home. It is the nature of human religions to offer both the truth as well as some misinterpretations. Regardless, all things work to good for those who love our Father.

Q: Is there any compelling evidence we humans can understand that validates the unconditionally loving nature of God?

A: Yes, for those who would listen. What other way of life is truly sustainable for all eternity than choosing unconditional love as our guide? Our free will guarantees there will be differences of opinion. In truth, an infinite number of potential conflicts exist at every moment. As has already been seen, some will choose selfishly, and those potential conflicts can become difficult situations. When selfishness continues to guide us, our differences become wars.

Q: But you have already said that we live in a lawful universe where we reap what we sow. Isn't there such a thing as "righteous recompense," where we (without sin) protect ourselves and our loved ones from transgressors who would harm us?

A: Can our Father or any of us be permanently harmed? Is there any sin that cannot be made right? Our true nature is in the perfect image of our Father. Jesus' resurrection was offered as proof that humans can do their worst for us, but no permanent harm will result if we live a life of unconditional love.

Q: What about being "wise as serpents yet harmless as doves?" Doesn't that include protecting yourself and those you love?

A: Yes, but remember who is included in our loving family. Which souls should we exclude from the list of those we desire to help and protect? I understand what you're saying, but let me offer a larger perspective.

You have had past lives where you were wrongfully persecuted and even killed. Not only you but those you loved suffered because of the selfish acts of others. However, how are you doing today? You are quite happy, have a wonderful family, are prosperous, and truly enjoy life. I can add that many of those who suffered from the mistreatment you experienced in those past lives are also a significant part of your life now. The more revealing question is, how much "permanent harm" was inflicted by those heinous crimes against you?

Q: That is an interesting perspective. You are correct that I don't feel "harmed" today even though you have told me that I was badly mistreated in the past. I'm not sure how to process this concept.

A: By realizing that no matter how awful something seems to us on Earth, the heavenly perspective is quite different. While greatly regrettable, the most heinous acts of humans are only steps off the path (for which we will reap what we've sown) until we freely choose a better, more loving way to live.

Q: You mentioned that unconditional love is the only sustainable way for us to get along in eternity. I'm beginning to see that any lesser approach than using love as the guide could keep us apart forever. We must forgive our transgressors to the point where no ill feelings exist. Only then can we return to trusting and loving each other. Once we are without sin and someone transgresses against us, we will say, "Forgive them, Father, for they know not what they do," and actually mean it to the very core of our being.

A: And that is His true nature manifested in the life of Jesus. It is also our true nature. We are simply in the process of remembering who we are and how loving we can become. When our choices are guided by fear, we are capable of great selfishness and destruction. Rest assured that if our fearful ways did manage to wipe out the human species, our loving Father would provide yet another way of escape from our selfish choices.

Q: In closing, can you offer words of encouragement regarding the true nature of God?

A: Whenever you feel sad or discouraged, think about these things. A place is already prepared for you that we may all be joyously together forever. When you accept His loving ways for your own, greater things than Jesus has done, you will do also. It is our Father's great pleasure to give us His kingdom. Be not afraid, for our Father loves you with an everlasting love. Lest we think otherwise, the Bible does indeed support that this is His true nature.

Helen Ruth

As with most people, my parents had a great deal of influence on my values and beliefs. My mother, Helen Ruth Schroeder, helped me find a spiritual course that has served me well. The story of her spiritual awakening is included in this book to help the reader better understand how I came to be who I am because of my mother.

Helen Ruth was born just shortly before the Great Depression began. She lived in Brooklyn with her parents, but they divorced when she was young, and neither one was able to care for her because of the nature of their employment. During her formative years, she was cared for by other family members when they could manage it and by a Catholic boarding school when the family could not. Needless to say, this did not offer the most loving and supportive upbringing a child could experience.

She was raised Catholic and devoted herself to that religion and its tenets. After the Depression eased and WWII ended, her father was able to send her to college. She chose the University of Texas with psychology as her major. There, she met my father and her future husband, Fred Schroeder. They dated for a few years and were married in 1951.

They arranged to spend their honeymoon at Lake Louise in Canada and began the long drive to get there the day after they were married. My father was trying to pass a slow-moving truck on a two-lane highway on a hill. When he finally did see the oncoming car, he could only swerve to the left into a ditch to avoid a collision. Their car came to an abrupt stop, throwing Fred against the steering wheel and causing him to lose consciousness. My mother was also dazed but could open the car door and stand up. When she did, the gas tank that had ruptured in the wreck exploded at that exact moment.

Helen Ruth was engulfed in the flames but quickly rolled onto the ground to extinguish them. She was able to get up and check on my father, who, having been unconscious during the explosion, was unaware of what had just happened.

A passerby called the authorities, and they called for an ambulance.

My mother was communicative but in shock and kept saying she was all right. The ambulance driver rushed my father to the hospital, thinking his ribs were broken. Helen Ruth followed the ambulance in a police car. On the way there, the burns Helen Ruth suffered started to discolor, showing the severity of the damage. She, too, was admitted once they arrived at the emergency room.

Her burns were extensive, causing her to be scarred for life over her face, arms, and legs. Anything that was not covered by the sun dress she was wearing had been burned in the explosion. Years later, I saw family pictures of the massive scabs on her body and the results of skin graft surgery, but those were taken months after she had been released from the hospital. She rarely spoke of those months of recovery, but her suffering must have been horrible.

She never lost her faith and never blamed God for her accident. She went on to start a family with Fred. My brother Bill was born first, and my sister Jan was born a year later. For a while, it seemed that Helen Ruth's life was finally on the path she had hoped for before the accident. Jan was only two months old when tragedy struck again.

My mother went to check on my sister early one morning and found her breathing but non-responsive. She would not wake up. A frantic trip to the emergency room led to many tests confirming that Jan had suffered a blood clot in the brain. It had deprived her of oxygen long enough to cause permanent damage. Jan would remain in a coma for the rest of her life. Her body was healthy, but my parents were told she would not regain consciousness.

The doctors counseled my parents that it would be better to place Jan in a professional care facility rather than have them care for her at home. They thought that even if my mother could adequately care for Jan, it would be a burden on Bill and any future children if their sister lived with them in her condition. Neither of my parents wanted to be separated from

Jan like that, but following the doctors' advice, they made the arrangements for Jan's professional care.

I was born in 1955 when Jan was two years old. The family still lived in Texas then, and my mother underwent a significant spiritual change. Two events finally separated her from the Catholic Church, but not from her belief in a loving God. One was that a priest told her she could not take communion on any day when she followed her doctor's advice of eating a few saltine crackers first thing in the morning. The doctor's suggestion was given to relieve the morning sickness she had during her pregnancy with me. The priest pointed out that "God's rules" were more important than "doctor's orders." Her other encounter with the Catholic Church was much more significant.

The counsel she received from another priest regarding what happened to Jan was my mother's primary source of discontent. The priest stated that the reason behind Jan's affliction was a mystery, but that my mother should rest assured that it was meant to serve the greater glory of God. Helen Ruth couldn't imagine God desiring to be glorified through her daughter's and the family's suffering.

Those events convinced Helen Ruth that her answers would not be found in the Catholic Church. Being a voracious reader, she started looking to other religions for the answers she sought. A friend recommended a book entitled "*There is a River*" written by Thomas Sugrue. It was a biography of the life of Edgar Cayce. Cayce was one of the most notable psychics in this country and perhaps the best-documented psychic in the world.

The life story of Cayce was factually compelling and also convinced my mother of the accuracy of the metaphysical information Cayce's readings offered. At the end of the book was a chapter entitled *Philosophy.* It offered a world view from the perspective of Cayce's readings describing the nature of God and our relationship with Him. My mother felt she had finally found answers to the questions of her heart. She shared the book with my father, and he agreed with her. For the rest of

Helen Ruth's life, there was no greater devotee to the psychic readings of Edgar Cayce and the non-profit organization that survived him.

In 1959, my mother made her first visit to Virginia Beach, Virginia. That is where the headquarters for Edgar Cayce's Association for Research and Enlightenment (A.R.E.) is located. She met many people she had read about in *There is a River*. During most of his psychic readings, Helen Ruth enjoyed one person in particular, Gladys Davis Turner, Cayce's stenographer. After Cayce died in 1945, Gladys made it her life's work to cross-index the readings and make them available to everyone. Because of my mother's appetite for the Cayce readings, she was in regular contact with Gladys long after her initial visit to A.R.E. headquarters.

Soon after that, my father was offered a better job in California. He and my mother decided to move, but that reopened the question of caring for Jan. Against their intuitive feelings, they again agreed Jan should be cared for by professionals. They decided to relocate her to a nearby care facility in California. That night, Helen Ruth had a dream that changed everything.

She dreamed she was reading a book and noticed the page number in the corner. Even though she couldn't remember what she read, the page number stuck out because my mother was sure it was an index number for an Edgar Cayce reading. She called Gladys Davis Turner the next day and asked if she could be sent a copy of the reading with that index number. Since Gladys was used to my mother's requests for readings, she didn't ask anything else and said she'd get back to her soon.

When Gladys called back, she was very curious to find out why my mother had asked for that particular reading. She was curious because it had never been transcribed from Gladys' shorthand dictation, meaning it had not yet been available to the public. That made it nearly impossible for my mother to have known the reading existed and asked for it.

When Helen Ruth said that she had received the reading number in a dream, Gladys responded that the information should prove interesting because it seemed the universe had gone to great lengths to ensure she received it.

When the transcribed Cayce reading arrived in the mail, my mother read it immediately. The person who requested the reading also had a child whose comatose condition was similar to Jan's. The questions followed much of what my mother wanted to know regarding whether Jan should be cared for professionally or if they should care for her at home. The answers opened up a new perspective regarding people in Jan's position.

The Cayce reading said that even though such people don't have a physical consciousness, the soul "hovers" about the body and is very much aware of everything that occurs in thought or action around them. The reading clarified that the parents should try to communicate with the child, knowing that the soul will be aware of their thoughts and love. Whether they should care for the child themselves or leave that to the professionals, the reading said that was their choice. However, while it would be more challenging to care for the child at home, that was where the child would receive greater love and attention.

Helen Ruth didn't hesitate to tell Fred about the reading, and they agreed that they would bring Jan home and care for her there once they relocated to California. They were relieved to have such loving confirmation of their intuitive feelings, especially when it went against the advice of the medical professionals. Within a few weeks of my parents making this decision, Jan passed away unexpectedly from pneumonia.

I never saw Jan in person because she had lived in a care facility and died when I was very young. But the lessons I learned from hearing this story have served me well. I learned that others receive our thoughts as surely as our ears hear and our eyes see. We subconsciously communicate with others in ways that do not require the five senses, even if we consciously ignore them.

I also learned of the great sacrifices we can choose to make in helping others. No doubt Jan had her own lessons learned through the seven years she was attached to her unconscious body. But once my parents understood that they could communicate with Jan regardless of appearances, my sister was free to move on. I was awestruck to know Jan was willing to put herself in that limited existence for so many years to help my family grow in understanding that we are all eternally connected.

These lessons and beliefs have been the foundation that helped me become who I am today. While I have studied many spiritual paths, I find that I believe nothing conflicts with a God of unconditional love or with the overall philosophy offered in the Edgar Cayce readings.

Pre-existence of the Soul

Q: Many religions have different accounts of the origin of the soul. While much agreement exists that God created us all, disagreement arises regarding when the soul was created. Just how old are we?

A: How many years old is anyone who lives for eternity? We are created in our Father's image. We have no beginning and will have no end.

Q: So the soul does not come into existence with the creation of the human form. If we have no beginning, as you said, does that mean God did not create us?

A: This concept is difficult to define with a limited understanding of time and space. Our Father created us all, but for eternal beings, nothing precedes anything else. The closest concept you have with your finite human understanding is that our Father is the First Cause, and we all live and move and have our very being within the mind of His infinite love and creativity. After eternal beings come everything else that is created sequentially as measured by time. So, eternal creations precede everything that has a beginning. To close the loop I just opened, everything with a beginning also has an end.

Q: It is hard enough to understand that God has no beginning. It is even harder to understand that we, too, have no beginning, and yet we were created by God. Can you reconcile all that so it makes sense to my finite mind?

A: Let's start with the concept that things having a beginning must also have an end. A good analogy would be the difference between our daily lives on Earth and playing virtual video games on the internet. Imagine that our human lives are analogous to our eternal existence as souls and internet video games are all the physical ways we can live and interact together within space and time. Internet video games have a definite beginning and will end at some point when we lose interest in playing them. Our eternal/human existence is not dependent upon the internet, though many are so enmeshed in it that they hardly live anywhere else.

Q: I understand that part, though I hadn't seen an addiction to the internet as analogous to being trapped in a human body on Earth before. I still don't get how God could be our Creator if we have no beginning or end.

A: It may help to consider the liquid metal element you call mercury. Watching the substance change its shape and form is fascinating, yet it is always unchanging because it is a base element like hydrogen. When we shake up a bit of mercury, it seems to divide into many tiny balls of silver. The substance can split and seamlessly merge at will. The tiniest ball of mercury is part of the whole and can be said to be created by the whole since all mercury is the same.

Q: That helped, but mercury doesn't have a unique consciousness to keep track of every part that separates and merges back together. Are you saying that we only have an awareness of being separate souls when we are apart from God?

A: No. Your point is where the analogy just given falls short. Our destiny as our Father's beloved children is to know ourselves to be ourselves and yet always one with the Whole. We are like eternal corpuscles in our Father's body, so to speak, very much aware of our uniqueness.

Q: But there had to be a first time when we all became separately conscious souls. Can't we say that moment was when we were all created?

A: You are understandably thinking according to the limitations of sequential time. If there is no time or space in our natural state of being, how can anything precede anything else? All of eternity happens in the same instance. Perhaps an earthly analogy will help with this concept.

Q: You can explain how God created us all, but we souls have always been and will always be? You should have started with that one.

A: Indeed, but you needed to get to this point to open your mind to the truth. Think back to your life science class in college. You watched a film showing an egg turning into a zygote and then starting to divide into separate cells within the walls of a single cell.

Q: I do remember that! It was fascinating to see the countless identical cells within the membrane of the original egg.

A: Can you see that the countless tiny cells within the original zygote are analogous to all souls being like corpuscles in the body of God?

Q: Yes, but I don't see how that helps. They still have a beginning.

A: Do they? Consider the creation event carefully for a moment. If the creation of souls took place before time or space existed, didn't all of the souls come into existence at the same time? Could you point to any of the cells within the original zygote and say that one is older than the other?

Q: No, but I can say that God preceded them all.

A: You will understand if you can follow a different image. Think of a square, blank piece of paper. Is the left side of the paper older or younger than the right side of the same page?

Q: I agree that every part of the paper is the same age. If you say the paper is analogous to being the zygote or God, I'm still with you.

A: Good. Now, mentally draw a tic-tac-toe grid on the blank page, then visualize the nine identical resulting squares waiting for the game to begin.

Q: I'm still with you.

A: As the game proceeds, each square takes on a unique role in how the game unfolds; some are blank, some have X's, and some have O's. Each square is a necessary part of the game regardless of the content it holds.

Q: Okay, but there is a sequence to each game played. A new game takes place when it's over until the players tire of it. Each game precedes all those that follow it.

A: Yes, but in this analogy, the squares are souls, and the paper is God. The contents of each square represent each soul's free will choices. In this way, the games have a beginning and will have an end. While viewed as individuals, the souls have always been and will always be a part of the paper, which in this analogy is God.

Q: I follow your words, but it leaves my head spinning. The implication is that God didn't just create us; each soul is a part of God. The only difference between each soul comes down to the free will choices we have made.

A: Exactly. God derives love and joy by seeing all of Creation through His beloved children's infinite eyes or perspectives. This is how the Creator remains happy, entertained, and even surprised throughout eternity. It is much the same with human parents and their children.

Q: How can I describe this concept to those who believe that each soul has a finite beginning? Many believe the soul is created upon human conception. I'm guessing the answer is 'no,' but is there some basis in truth for this belief?

A: Only that it is consistent with the basic Christian creed that the soul is created with the human body. That is a misinterpretation of the Bible's story of creation.

Q: I remember it saying we were all created in God's image in Chapter 1 of Genesis, and then Adam (humankind) was created in Chapter 2.

A: The Bible and Genesis are much closer to truth with that description, as you just gave, over how those verses are often interpreted. The Christian creed is consistent in denying the pre-existence of the soul, but that is not the truth. It would be more accurate to interpret "Adam's creation" as our eternal souls becoming connected to a physical body on Earth rather than believing our souls have a beginning at the moment of human conception or birth.

Q: What is the advantage of believing either way about the pre-existence of the soul?

A: The advantage to believing in the soul's pre-existence is knowing the truth that sets us free. The benefit of accepting the Christian creed is that we do not have to undo the selfishness we've created once we repent, as the creed defines such. This is not truly an advantage, but I'm answering from the same limited perspective you asked the question.

Q: Can you expand on that? I'm not sure what you mean.

A: There were two main agendas that led to the concept of being saved by accepting Jesus' sacrifice as the key to our salvation. The first was to remove all complexities from being saved for the uneducated masses. In that way, they could follow the role model example Jesus set without becoming lost in how or why Jesus did what He did.

Q: And the other agenda item was…?

A: That all spiritual interpretation should come from the church leadership. However, even with the best intentions, we should not dictate what is spiritually correct for others. If the church admitted that our souls existed before our human bodies, the door is opened to reincarnation. If we have all had past human lives, we must also take responsibility for our past choices. The moment we agree that a person has multiple human lives, the idea that a soul is saved forever the moment they accept Jesus as their Lord and Savior becomes moot. Church leaders, having long denied reincarnation exists, feel they will lose control of "spiritual interpretation" if they reverse themselves now and accept reincarnation as truth.

Q: But isn't the point of being on the Earth to follow the loving example Jesus set as the best path back to God? Even with reincarnation, isn't that the same as accepting and loving God (the Christ Spirit) as the highest authority?

A: I would agree, but ask a group of Southern Baptist ministers what is required for a soul's salvation, and you will likely get a very different answer than the one you just offered.

Q: But why allow so many conflicting answers regarding such an important question as our eternal salvation?

A: Your earthly justice system has a good answer to that. It is better to allow 10 guilty men to go free rather than wrongly convicting even one innocent person. When it comes to free will, it is better to allow for various conflicts in our spiritual beliefs rather than try to force anyone to believe something against their will.

Q: I can appreciate the value of free will, but aren't there ways of letting the truth be known on Earth that don't violate our ability to choose?

A: Our Father never misses an opportunity to do just that. This discussion is one of many ways to offer the truth to those with ears to hear. The truth is always available through asking in meditation, through discernment of the spiritual writings maintained through the ages, and primarily through life's lessons as we spiritually develop.

Q: It sounds as if you're saying that the Christian creed is misinterpreting the will and love of God. I know this question is a little off the subject, but is it a greater sin to misinterpret God's guidance compared to the other sins we commit? For example, are the televangelists who selfishly enrich themselves in the name of God any worse than the people who defraud others on Wall Street?

A: Since we are all a part of our loving Father, is there any sin we can commit where we have not misinterpreted His will for us? The answer to your question is not a simple yes or no. It comes down to how thoroughly each person intended to defraud others. We often assign the greatest blame to the person at the top, but there are occasions where the person in charge is altruistic, while others in the organization have a selfish agenda. This becomes more obvious when looking at our Father and His children.

Q: I am embarrassed to admit that I never thought about how I was misrepresenting God when I made poor choices. That's a perspective I want to remember the next time I consider which path to take.

A: While that can be helpful to remember, nothing good comes from lowering your self-image. Recognize and follow what you see as a better way to live at each opportunity. Our Father is not anxious that we represent Him properly. He patiently guides and encourages us, each at our own pace. While the soul is eternal, our selfish choices had a beginning and will also have an end.

Q: In closing, do you have further words of encouragement or guidance to share that hasn't come up in the questions I asked?

A: Never doubt your place in our Father's kingdom as His beloved child. There is nothing more precious to our Father than you. Though we might not fully understand, this cherished status we have in His family is shared by every soul. Does that make us any less beloved by Him? No. That would be impossible.

He is all-knowing, and our Father never stops loving you as His treasured eternal companion and co-creator. He does not make mistakes and is an excellent judge of character. This experience of separation from Him is but a minor blip on the screen compared to the joy you bring Him in eternity. Our Father already sees the endless glorious experiences ahead for us all. No matter how we go astray, always believe you are worth the wait!

Marshall

Before I retired as a captain in the Army Reserve in 1989, I had the chance to serve in several countries. One of the perks of international training exercises was discovering local craftsmanship—like in South Korea, where I once had high-quality custom suits made for a fraction of the U.S. price.

Over those years, I built lasting friendships with people from all walks of military life. One of the closest was Marshall, a dependable and good-humored sergeant in my section. We shared years of service, laughter, and stories. So when Marshall called one day to say he'd be heading to South Korea, I was happy to hear from him.

My wife and I had just rebranded our no-alcohol teen nightclub to "Zzapp." The memory of South Korea's affordable embroidery and tailoring came flooding back, and Marshall offered an idea: he could have custom jackets for the club featuring our new logo. It seemed like a great opportunity. I handed him $1,500 in cash—enough for a dozen jackets made to order—and he promised to return with them in about a month.

But weeks passed, and there was no sign of Marshall—or the jackets. I left messages with no response. Finally, I contacted Jim, a mutual acquaintance who had traveled with him. Jim was initially evasive but eventually called back with something I wasn't unprepared for.

He told me Marshall had developed a drug problem. Jim had witnessed it firsthand during their trip and admitted Marshall had done nothing to get the jackets made. Most of the money, he explained, had been used to buy drugs. Marshall, too ashamed to face me, had asked Jim to break the news before he did.

When Marshall finally called, his voice was low and filled with remorse. He promised to repay the money. I wasn't happy, but I told him I understood. We ended the call on that note—uneasy but not unkind.

A couple of weeks later, Jim called again. This time, the news shattered me. Marshall had died by suicide the night before.

It was a violent and tragic end. While I knew the money was gone, that loss faded into insignificance. I couldn't stop thinking about the man I'd known for years—the loyal, upbeat friend who had never shown a hint of despair. I replayed our memories, searching for signs I might've missed.

I had never personally known someone who took their own life before. Hearing about suicide is one thing. Losing someone you knew, laughed with, or served with changes how you see the world.

My metaphysical beliefs helped me navigate the aftermath. I let go of the anger over the money, believing that Marshall now faced greater reckonings beyond this life. Instead, I turned my grief into prayer, lifting his spirit up in hope and compassion.

In the chapter that follows, I explore the spiritual dimensions of abortion and suicide—topics that challenge us deeply but, perhaps, offer a chance to understand the soul's journey with more grace and wisdom.

Abortion & Suicide

Q: I wanted to ask about two very controversial issues: abortion and suicide. Am I correct in linking these two, or should they be handled separately?

A: They have similar points to discuss regarding the sanctity of life, but the motivations for each often differ in specifics beyond selfishness and fear. Why don't you start with one, and we'll see how it develops?

Q: Is there ever a time and circumstance when having an abortion is the correct answer to the question of an unwanted pregnancy?

A: Yes, but so much of that answer concerns the parents' perspective.

Q: Does the parents' perspective change the morality of having an abortion?

A: Yes. For example, if the parents believe abortion is always wrong, then having the baby is the only morally correct choice available. If the parents feel that abortions have their place in the world, then they might make another choice and remain faithful to what they believe

Q: But if an abortion is killing a baby, how does the morality of that change with their perspective?

A: Abortion does kill a gestating physical body but not the soul. If the life of that physical form is so precious to the parents that they believe abortion is wrong, then they (not our Father) condemn themselves on that basis. Suppose their perspective is that the incoming soul is only deprived of that particular body to enter the Earth, and they will still be able to be born as a human in another body at another time. In that case, that is a different moral circumstance. Our Father judges neither perspective, even though we might strongly condemn ourselves and others for such choices.

Q: This sounds like the line between right and wrong is relative. Is that correct?

A: No, but this is mainly because of semantics. The line between right and wrong, as you called it, is separated by our intentions, be they loving or selfish. Laws made by humans most often require acting in a certain way no matter what we think. The laws made by our Father ask that we use love to guide our thoughts and actions.

Q: Can you give me an example?

A: Of course. All notes played on a piano have the potential to make beautiful music or ugly noise. Think of the notes played together in a song as combining our choices in life. Notes played together with a loving intent make beautiful music. Notes chosen with a selfish intent are not in harmony with our Father's creation. There are no wrong notes, but there is always potential harmony or discord in our choices. How much beauty we add to our Father's creation is measured by the love we manifest, not by what we do or what is accomplished, as humankind measures such.

Q: So choosing an abortion when you think it is wrong is what causes the discord, not the actual abortion itself?

A: Yes, if no other circumstances exist to consider.

Q: Then the answer to my question on the morality of abortion often depends on a person's belief in the pre-existence of the soul. Is that right?

A: Correct. If the parents believe that the soul pre-exists and survives the body, then abortion is perceived and judged much differently than if the parents believe that the soul and the body come into existence at the same time.

Q: So when were we created?

A: Before the beginning, as humankind thinks of such things. Our Father desired to share His love, joy, and glory by creating a family of souls in His perfect image. Our Father gave us all free will to choose against His loving ways and conditional unlimited access to His knowledge and power. The only thing we lack, if you can call it such, is experience. Our free will, by definition, requires that our experiences are chosen by us rather than already having them programmed into us.

Q: So we made selfish choices that resulted in our separation from God in consciousness. Living on the Earth in these human bodies has tools we now use to help us remember and accept His loving ways for our own. Doesn't the Bible support the pre-existence of the soul? I remember reading that we were first created in God's image, and then the next chapter tells of Adam's creation and breathing the soul into the body.

A: That is not how many on Earth would interpret those verses, but you are correct.

Q: So let's say the parents believe in the soul's pre-existence and reincarnation. Neither of them considers having an abortion is murder. Is there a circumstance where an abortion would be the wrong choice for them?

A: Many. When is it right to use abortion as a birth control device instead of taking the proper contraceptive precautions? When is it right to abort a child because they are not the gender their parents wanted? The list goes on like that.

Q: What about aborting a baby that the doctors have told you will be born with severe challenges in the brain or function of the body? Add to those scenarios that the birth of the child puts the mother's life at risk.

A: Such circumstances call for much prayer and meditation as the best way to discern the answer. Many reasons exist for such challenging babies forming, so either answer could be correct given all the factors involved.

Q: What would be an example of negative karma one might experience if they selfishly choose to abort?

A: Often, that can manifest as not being able to have children in another life when they are truly desired. Others can experience, while not in physical form, how the perfect body and circumstance for them to enter this Earth and grow spiritually is denied because the soul's potential human parents aborted the fetus. There are others, but those are the easiest to understand.

Q: Are there circumstances where choosing not to have an abortion is wrong?

A: That is more difficult to describe. This can happen when a soul comes in to do specific work and ends up sidetracked because of an unplanned pregnancy. Imagine if that had been Jesus. How different would the world be now if He had chosen to live that life as a good parent, providing for His family's needs instead of completing what He came in to do?

Q: Would that have ruined everything forever?

A: No. If He had made such a choice, it would have delayed the arrival of Christ incarnate on Earth until another lifetime. However, even if another perfected soul had to step up to take on the role of the Christ incarnate, our Father would not have denied His children such essential guidance in how to return Home.

Q: I guess that answers my next question about Joseph and Mary choosing to abort baby Jesus and the impact that might have had on humanity.

A: I'll answer it anyway for those who might not make the connection. From a human perspective, our selfish choices can delay the universe's return to balance, but how long can we thwart the loving ways of our Father? If Jesus' human parents had decided to abort His body, the birth of the Christ incarnate would have inevitably occurred at the next opportunity. If humankind's combined choices create a vacuum attracting such a loving spiritual leader, the universe will never stop working to fill that void. When our desires align with God's, nothing in the universe can stand in our way forever.

Q: Is that saying that Hitler and Stalin were filling a leadership void we humans desired?

A: That's one way of putting it, or those two souls would not have come into their positions of power. We always have free will and can change the conditions that attract such challenging leaders. Only those things in accord with our Father's loving ways are eternal and virtually inevitable. The suffering that comes from our selfish choices has a beginning, and those things will end. Only love is everlasting.

Q: Those sound like other topics to explore later, such as Hitler and Stalin and the beginning/end concept you just mentioned.

A: We, indeed, will speak of them again.

Q: Then let's switch topics now to suicide. Is suicide ever the correct choice to make?

A: Let me set the stage for this issue with Jesus' life as the example. Because Jesus knew that He was likely to be killed if He allowed Himself to be taken by the Romans, couldn't that be considered a suicide? What about people who purposefully provoke the police, knowing they will respond with deadly force? Isn't that known as committing "suicide by cop?"

Q: You're saying Jesus' death on the cross was a suicide?

A: Depending on how you define that word, it surely could have been. After all, He did foresee all the outcomes of allowing Himself to be taken by the Romans. Jesus knew in Gethsemane that there was almost a 100% certainty that He would be tortured and killed if He remained in Jerusalem. Is "suicide by Roman soldier" any different from "suicide by cop?"

Q: But there was so much riding on what occurred with Jesus that it hardly seems like He was running away from life. It must have been quite the opposite, wasn't it?

A: Indeed, but the point you're now making is the shared concept between abortion and suicide I wanted to illustrate. Purposefully giving up our lives is neither right nor wrong. It still comes down to our reasons and motivations for making such a choice.

Q: Well, I'm guessing the most typical motive for committing suicide is that people find living on Earth so unbearable that they believe whatever comes next can't be any worse. Can suicide with such hopelessness as the motivation be the right choice?

A: Not as you worded the question, but let me again switch examples to Jesus' death by crucifixion. It usually takes a few days for a victim of crucifixion to die. That is typically due to suffocation because of the legs' inability to take the stress off the collapsing lungs. Jesus separated from His body at the earliest moment He could, seeing there was no purpose in His continued suffering. That's when He was quoted as saying, "It is finished." If any human makes the choice to end their life knowing there is little more to be gained, that is not a selfish reason to die. Before you ask, we should discern what is correct through prayer and meditation to be sure it is the right choice.

Q: Great answer! But what of the person who takes their life, like Hitler did, to avoid the consequences of all they had done to get to that horrible point?

A: As I mentioned in the case of an inappropriate abortion, from a human perspective, we can only delay reaping what we've sown, not avoid it altogether. The person who commits suicide to avoid suffering due to their past actions has only made their challenges more difficult to overcome in the future.

Q: Is that because they will reincarnate, and their life circumstances will unfold so they will build up to the same unbearable point again?

A: Often, yes, and with each suicide, the pattern of running away by killing ourselves is reinforced. It may be difficult to understand this, but suicide becomes addictive when chosen to avoid our negative karma. The suicidal pattern can become reinforced in each new life, making the original challenge that brought about our extreme suffering even more difficult to overcome.

Q: What is it like for a person who selfishly commits suicide when they arrive on the "other side?"

A: Most see immediately when they've made the wrong choice. Without the limitations of the conscious mind, a larger picture is realized: nothing has improved, and all that they've suffered in the life just ended begins anew, bringing them to the same pivotal point in a future life.

Q: I guess I'm having trouble understanding that. If the person taking their life immediately realizes their mistake, how does suicide become repeated and even addictive?

A: It looks so easy from the other side to avoid making this mistake again. Without the distractions of the earthly world and body, we clearly see what we want to accomplish and how to do so. Our perspective changes once we incarnate as humans, and the distractions begin. As we lose contact with our higher mind, we cut ourselves off from receiving direct help from the mental and spiritual realms. The tools of love, patience, and cooperation are pushed aside. Eventually, we are back in the same predicament that led to our past suicide.

Q: This may sound odd, but given that many people prefer to run away from their problems, why isn't suicide more common than it is?

A: The normal human instinct for self-preservation helps here, especially when we cut ourselves off from the mental and spiritual aspects of our being. Fear is another reason suicide isn't more popular. We are afraid of the unknown and especially of what awaits us after the death of the body. There is another reason suicide lacks greater popularity, and it's not the joke it will first appear to be. That's because people in such a stymied frame of mind tend to procrastinate. A lack of focus and direction in life also works to delay most decisions we make, even to kill our bodies.

Q: I can guess that in this case, procrastination keeps us alive long enough for our life circumstances to improve to the point where we change our minds.

A: Occasionally, but this is a good time to bring up how much help surrounds us all at every moment. While in human form, we are constantly surrounded by guides (helpful souls) and angels whose purpose is to support, encourage, and help us get the most from our lives. Any delay in killing ourselves gives all those helpers on the "other side" a chance to assist in calming the mind and fears of the suffering soul.

Q: Having all that help from the other side is a very comforting thought. It also brings me to the difficult subject of those people with afflicted minds. If someone has Dementia or Alzheimer's, is suicide or euthanasia ever advisable in such cases where the mind is failing or perhaps has already failed?

A: This is indeed a difficult subject. It is up to the individual to make that choice before they can no longer do so. Given the current secular laws, no effort should be made by a loved one to take it upon themselves to end the suffering of another, even when they are afflicted in this manner. That is why we should make our intentions known ahead of time, much like we do through a living will.

Q: What is it like for the soul of a mentally challenged human to experience such an impaired mortal life as that?

A: Very limiting. Imagine that every time you slept, you dreamed you were in jail and had few privileges. In this case, the soul experiences similar confinement and isolation when connected to an afflicted human body and brain. This is especially true when the body is in a waking state.

Q: What happens to the soul when the body is asleep?

A: The soul has more latitude to travel when the body is at rest. In fact, the soul travels most often during R.E.M. sleep when the body is dreaming. The conscious memories or dreams we humans have are the best recollections our minds can retain of our souls' experiences beyond the Earth's three dimensions.

Q: So a comatose patient is hardly a burden to the soul that is attached to that body?

A: Not as you're thinking right now. The soul has the ability to travel more often when the body is not conscious, but even that is not without its limitations. A reasonable analogy would be the difference between watching a sporting event on

TV versus being at the event in person. The soul usually travels more freely when not attached to a body, but it is not fully vested in other realms as long as the body lives on Earth.

Q: So, does a soul experience life when unconscious in human form, as though in jail with unlimited cable channels to watch?

A: You know you're being facetious now, but that description is close enough to the truth to work.

Q: It seems like we often outlive our body's usefulness. Why don't our bodies die when they're supposed to for our highest spiritual growth?

A: If no other factors were involved, that is largely how it works. There is no reason to stop learning and growing as long as we're alive in or out of a body. However, we often stop progressing in our later years, though we only cheat ourselves by not trying to improve.

From an eternal perspective, if we choose to live "extra years" on Earth in human form because we're afraid of death or due to other mundane reasons, what have we lost? On the other hand, people "will" themselves to die all the time. We might say something like, "They died of a broken heart," but the truth is often that they willed their body to stop living.

Q: Is "willing ourselves to die" a form of suicide? Assuming it is, is that always an acceptable method of taking our own lives without becoming addicted to it?

A: In truth, there is no difference between willing yourself to die and physically arranging your own death. The motivations and any resulting karma follow the same rules. Most people don't think of maintaining a poor diet as being so bad, but not following a healthy lifestyle is in itself a form of slow suicide. From that perspective, virtually all humans start committing suicide not long after we are weaned.

Q: It does seem that abortion and suicide share similar moral choices even though they are two different issues. Do you have other helpful thoughts in closing?

A: Abortion and suicide have the same underlying challenges when it comes to the choices we make. The difference is that abortion is most often ending the life of another body, while suicide is ending our own human life. Both abortion and suicide can have their proper applications if we are making such choices out of love rather than fear or selfishness. The soul is never permanently harmed by anything we do, and that's important to keep in mind. We can never make such an awful choice that our Father cannot or will not joyously help us return Home.

This or Better

One of the toughest lessons I have learned this life came through a prosperity challenge. This was unusual for me, for I had already overcome a poverty consciousness and had been happily tithing to where I was spiritually fed for years. That I should again suffer financially after cheerfully and consistently following the laws of prosperity seemed unfair. It took a while for me to realize I was standing in my own way despite my prayers for help.

In the early 1980s, my wife Stephanie and I owned and operated a no-alcohol teenage nightclub in California. We had our financial ups and downs over the years with it, but things had been going well ever since we had learned to joyously give 10% of every dollar we made to people and organizations where we were spiritually nourished. When a well-funded competitor opened a beautiful club just a mile away from our location, the effect on our attendance and income was immediate and devastating. Our prosperous life took a tough turn, and we had to figure out how to get back on track.

Over the next several months, I developed a plan to turn things around successfully. The right people were helping me with the plan, but money was still a problem. I had none, and neither did anyone else I knew who would lend it to me under the circumstances. I finally realized that no matter how much I cut away at the plan to turn things around, I still needed about $15,000 as a minimum to implement it. The only way to get that much money together was to increase the club's attendance/revenues, so my prayers were focused on that specific goal.

Over the following months, several amazing things occurred that delayed my having to pay certain expenses. However, attendance continued to decline, so this did little to bring in additional cash. As grateful as I was for the constant financial reprieves, I kept asking God what purpose was served in delaying expenses if I didn't raise the $15,000. I was sure that if attendance didn't go up, the business couldn't survive.

Still, I tried to keep the doors open as long as possible. One of the last straws was to stop paying our liability insurance premiums. Our payments were incredibly high, $3,500 per month. Still, operating a business without liability insurance is a scary prospect. I knew I wouldn't have to worry for long because, at the rate business was falling, I had perhaps a few months more to operate before I could no longer pay the utilities and payroll. The attendance had to go up, or we'd have to close the doors.

At our bleakest point, the insurance company contacted me asking to audit our books. I assumed they thought I was being untruthful about the decline in business because my $3,500 monthly insurance premiums were based on the previous year's gross income. I had nothing to hide there, but it was a moot point if the attendance did not improve enough to save the business.

The insurance auditor came and went without saying much of anything. The following week, I finally made an appointment with a bankruptcy attorney to close the business down. But then I received a letter from the insurance company one day before that appointment. In the letter, they acknowledged that their audit confirmed the decline in our revenues. They thanked me for my business and enclosed a refund check for $15,300. I was stunned and delighted all at the same time.

I had forgotten that my insurance payments were based on the previous year's attendance and revenues when business was still quite good. I had been overpaying them for months regarding the actual premiums owed because our current attendance and income were much lower than the previous year. The money needed to execute the plan had been miraculously provided. As I was sure would happen, the club prospered better than ever after making those planned changes.

The greatest lesson for me was finally discovering why I was having financial trouble in the first place. I was "telling" God how I should be helped. I kept insisting that attendance had to go up for me to get the needed money. As I looked at the insurance refund check, I realized the reason I received the money I needed was that attendance had gone down instead of up.

So, I learned a tough lesson about not attempting to tie God's hands in how He can help resolve our challenges. I no longer insist that my prayers be answered only as I direct. Whenever I ask for anything in prayer, I am open to accepting His best solution (worded in prayer as "this, or better") as an improvement to my own ideas in resolving the challenge.

Prosperity

Q: Most self-help programs focus on improving relationships, health, and prosperity. I believe that prosperity is often the toughest lesson to learn of those three. Is that a correct assumption?

A: Yes. The concept and understanding of Oneness as it relates to prosperity is a great challenge for most people to apply in their lives.

Q: Why is that?

A: With health, connecting the "cause and effect" of how we treat and nourish our bodies with our physical well-being is easier. Regarding relationships, most people agree that the challenges between two or more people are best resolved within ourselves rather than thinking we can change anyone else.

Q: How does prosperity offer a more formidable challenge than we experience with health or relationships?

A: The "cause and effect" of what we do to change our level of prosperity is not so easily understood. Many believe that a person's prosperity is due to luck or that others are in greater control of their lives than themselves.

Q: Well, I understand that luck mostly reaps what we have sown. However, isn't how prosperous we are often in the hands of others?

A: It doesn't have to be, but when we give up our free will to choose, the free will of others often fills that void.

Q: That is a new concept for me. Are you saying that if we do not exercise our free will, the free will of others takes control of our lives?

A: Not exactly, but let's continue on this track, for it does lead to an important point.

Q: As usual, an example would be helpful here.

A: Think of our lives as a jigsaw puzzle where each new part of life's puzzle intersects and connects us all. The pieces we add to building the puzzle are similar to our choices. As the puzzle's picture unfolds, each new piece (choice) fills in more space.

Q: I can envision that pretty easily. What happens when our individual "puzzles" intersect or connect with others?

A: Then, the new pieces created by each person's choices fit together accordingly, with some fitting better than others. This is easiest to understand when one person comes into the life of another like a whirlwind and suddenly takes over the picture. It is not that one person's free will is greater than another's, but some choose to expand and take charge while others react to life instead of directing it.

Q: Is being a more assertive person the better way to live, or should we be more passive in our choices?

A: Neither approach is consistently right or wrong. They are simply the extremes used in illustrating this point.

Q: The point is that the choices "not made" by the submissive person put the assertive person's choices in greater control of how life will unfold for both of them.

A: Indeed. This is not always a bad thing; in fact, it is preferred in many cases. For instance, parents who allow their children to essentially raise themselves are not doing anyone a favor. However, when life is not unfolding according to our best interests, remaining submissive yet complaining about others does not help anyone.

Q: A frequent first step in being prosperous is to stop complaining and do something about the conditions we want to improve.

A: Correct, but often, people need specific advice beyond that to be of help. Many people know they don't like where they are but have no idea how to improve things. Developing a plan works better than blindly taking action without knowing where we're headed.

Q: Okay, so what's the plan?

A: First, it helps to define what prosperity truly is. Most people limit that definition to their wealth, but in truth, it encompasses the well-being of our wealth, health, and relationships. We will not have attained a prosperous balance until we are "content but not satisfied" in all aspects of our lives. Being content is good. Being satisfied hinders our growth because we lack the motivation to improve.

Q: Does that mean that some wealthy people are not prosperous?

A: Correct. Some of the most tragic figures in the news are wealthy celebrities or sports stars who demonstrate only too well that wealth alone does not resolve our challenges.

Q: If we are to be as prosperous as God, wouldn't that mean we're all supposed to be gazillionaires? I don't remember historical accounts saying Jesus had great wealth.

A: You are correct if you mean Jesus didn't have huge bank accounts, livestock, and land holdings. However, He lacked for nothing and attracted all the wealth required to help Him accomplish what He came to do. It would have become available if Jesus had needed great sums of money to do what our Father suggested.

Q: So, what is the best quick advice you can give for those three areas of prosperity? Start with health.

A: The balance we should seek with health is to match our assimilations with our eliminations. If we eat the right foods and exercise according to our body's needs to eliminate what it has taken in, then the body's health is assured, except for the effects on the mind. In that, too, we must maintain a balance of positive, loving thoughts, or the mind works against the good health of the body.

Q: I like that quick advice. How can we become more prosperous in our relationships?

A: By always recognizing the Oneness of all things. Be the changes we desire in others. Purposefully call out to the best within them as we role model our best and loving behavior. Always being patient and choosing to cooperate with others helps lead us to a win/win scenario that works best for all concerned. Not everyone will maintain a good relationship with us, but we should let that be their choice, not ours.

Q: Please continue with how we can prosper more with our wealth.

A: We should remember that prosperity in the form of wealth is our divine right. We must balance what we receive with what we give to claim it. That includes what we have and give in money, time, and skills.

Q: Does that mean we must give away everything we have regarding our money, time, and skills?

A: Yes, but not in the way you're thinking. I'll offer specifics on the concept of giving in a moment. In truth, we always give away 100% of the worldly possessions we receive, just not at every moment. We come into the earth without anything but our souls' experience and that's exactly what we leave with when the body dies.

Q: It's easy to lose sight of that when our only memories are the human ones between birth and death. What specifics can you offer about giving?

A: The ongoing giving in our lives can rightly be called a tithe or giving a tenth of all our gifts and earnings. Such giving needs to be offered from our time, skills, and wealth, and it should be given back to the sources of our spiritual nourishment.

Q: I can see writing checks to our place of worship, the Red Cross, or even the Humane Society, but I'm not clear on what you mean by giving our time and skills. Is that speaking mainly of volunteering?

A: It is, but there is much more to it than that. Giving our time to help feed the hungry and homeless is great. Even better is to serve others by helping through what we do best. For instance, if you are in the grocery business, cooking food for everyone who comes to partake is one thing. But what if you used your connections in the industry to get a great deal of food donated that the non-profit organization would otherwise have to pay to receive?

Q: I get it! Many people have the skills to help cook and serve food to the homeless, but not everyone can use those same volunteer hours to bring more food to the project. We should look at not just being of service, per se, but being of the greatest service we can use all the skills we possess.

A: You really did get it. The gifts or skills our Father bestows upon us are not only to be shared but also to be used wisely. For instance, Jesus is a great carpenter, but His time is often better spent sharing ideas with others, as we are doing here. That said, maintaining the right balance in all things is the key to prosperity. If we are so busy serving spiritually and mentally that the physical is ignored, that imbalance alone can hinder our prosperity.

Q: Serving spiritually? What does that mean?

A: Simply put, you should pray for others and visualize the best outcomes for everyone you encounter. This, too, is part of balanced giving.

Q: How do we know when the right balance has been reached?

A: When there is joy and service in all that we do, not only does everyone come out ahead because of our efforts, but we also feel energized and refreshed in the process. It's not that we cannot become tired at the end of the day, but being in balance means that we always have an enthusiasm for life and truly enjoy participating as an active part of the Whole.

Q: If that defines prosperity, then few people have it, or at least many fall short of that standard much of the time.

A: In that statement, we see a better path ahead. Giving a tithe of our time, skill, and wealth is sustainable with an appropriate plan. Start the day in prayer and meditation. When we do, our hearts and minds are open to our Father's suggestions that will help us achieve our goals.

Q: But that sounds like it covers much more than our donations to worthy causes and individuals. Are you suggesting we plan all of our activities around our giving?

A: We do this already, but often without thinking of it as giving, let alone following a prosperity plan. How perfect it would be if we never lost sight of the fact that we are giving when we work, socialize, exercise, eat, worship, vote, or pay bills. With an attitude of love, we constantly give and serve others in all we do.

Q: So "giving" should not be limited to a tenth of our time, skill and income?

A: Giving a tenth of all we receive in those areas ensures that our tithing extends beyond paying our bills or serving as an employee at our jobs. To give a tenth of all we are given, specifically to where we're spiritually fed, is just another bullet point on the "staying in balance" checklist. Everything we do with a loving and positive intention is serving. Ensuring that our donations of time, talent, and money support the activities that spiritually feed us ensures this wonderful cycle continues, especially where it works best.

Q: It sounds like where we worship should be high on our tithing list. However, how much should we give our preferred non-religious organizations of great service?

A: Asking in prayer and meditation will let you know. You will always be given those answers intuitively whenever you seek them with a loving heart.

Q: You speak of giving with joy, but when we're hurting for money, what joy is there in giving away what we already lack? I'm speaking of donating money rather than time and skill here.

A: A couple of metaphors might help to understand the challenge in what you ask. How can we take more life-giving oxygen into our bodies if we never exhale? To not give as we receive can figuratively, if not literally, choke the life out of us. If we clutch so tightly to what little money we have, what can we do to receive more? Unless we unclench our fists, we cannot open our hands (or minds) to accept His abundance.

Q: Well, it could still work if we have so little money that we can hold it in one hand and take in more with the other, couldn't it?

A: Clever idea, but realize your question already started with an impoverished mindset. It would work far better to ask, "How can we live without fear?" rather than asking, "How can we receive without giving?"

Q: How do we give without fear?

A: That depends on where each person is in their own mind. In truth, we are all divine children of our loving Father, sharing in His endless abundance. The moment we are unclear on that point, "fearless giving" becomes more difficult with each selfish choice we make. To turn that around, we need to start donating any amount where we can still have joy in the giving. Once the pattern of giving with joy is established, the amount we give can grow along with our faith in the laws of prosperity.

Q: What is the role of faith when it comes to prosperity and giving?

A: When we feel impoverished, we commonly believe we do not deserve to be prosperous. Faith in this regard is knowing that we deserve every good thing that happens to us and that our Father will provide all we ask for in love. If we let go of our fear and poverty consciousness, grace resolves whatever "lack" is karmically due to us.

Q: How does grace work in this case?

A: Grace means we will no longer suffer from any negative karma due to us the moment we truly learn our lesson. After all, if our suffering is only intended to be instructive, why would it continue after it has served its purpose?

Q: That makes sense. Are there additional reasons we fear giving other than not having enough for ourselves and our families?

A: Any number of them. We can feel we should not make more money than our parents because we hold them as the standard for many good things in our lives. We can feel giving is unethical because we are honor-bound to pay our secular bills first. Those who could otherwise tithe with joy stumble in fear because they feel they would be breaking a promise to those they owe.

Q: That last one is very real and not often discussed. How can we overcome the fear that we must make unethical choices to become prosperous?

A: That's a great question, for it covers many beliefs that conflict with the laws of prosperity. We should remember that giving in love, without reservation, is always ethical. Once we learn that lesson, our Father provides all we require and more to live a prosperous life.

Q: So you're saying that tithing when you can't pay the rent is okay? I think most landlords would disagree. Most people feel that God will be more understanding of us not tithing than a landlord would be of missing a rent payment.

A: While that is almost always true, there is a great way to work through the seeming paradoxes that can block a prosperity consciousness.

Q: Please explain what you meant by "seeming paradoxes." Do you mean that we must give with joy to be prosperous even though it is giving away what we don't have that makes us fearful in the first place? That is a challenge.

A: Achieving a prosperous life requires study and planning on two levels. For example, we must first learn the laws of aerodynamics before designing an airplane that can fly. Secondly, no matter how much we know about aerodynamics, the aircraft won't leave the ground without a proper design. So, knowing the laws of prosperity is not enough. We must also develop a workable plan, or our prosperous life will never get off the ground.

Q: I've got the picture, but how does that all work in real life?

A: First, learn the laws of prosperity. Then, figure out how to improve the design of our lives so we prosper or "fly." To do that, we may feel guided to change jobs or careers. We may feel moved to develop a product or service to sell. We might think of a new or better way to do what we already do. Prayer and meditation will always help us discern the best direction.

Q: So, can you offer a list of the laws of prosperity?

A: The list is lengthy if it is comprehensive. This is one area where clear, written instructions on the laws of prosperity are readily available. An author who has specialized in this is Catherine Ponder, though she has a traditional Christian approach that may not appeal to all. Self-help prosperity books and programs appeal to most people's interests and backgrounds. If we lovingly seek help and ask to be spiritually led, we will find what we need.

Q: Let's say I start tithing but don't get results after several weeks. If I only become more fearful of giving, how can I ever learn to be prosperous, let alone maintain the overall balance you spoke of before?

A: Once we start on the path to prosperity, we often find ourselves in a position where we want to give, but our fear holds us back. Our desires and choices will always attract and create conditions to overcome this fearful block. A common fear is the feeling that the amount we give won't be enough. The size of our gift is hardly the point. Letting go of the fear and feeling joy in the giving is the better measure of progress in this most difficult lesson. How much we choose to "live without" before we understand this truth is a matter of time and free will. We are all destined to be prosperous. How long that takes is up to us.

Q: So, is a "prosperity consciousness" like a bank refusing to lend us money until we no longer need it?

A: I would have phrased it differently, but many will closely identify with your words. The truth is that even if we were given all the wealth we desired, without maintaining a prosperous balance in our thoughts and actions, true prosperity will continue to elude us. Our health, relationships, and/or wealth will always falter without consistently using love as our guide.

Q: A common fear is that we might start tithing for selfish reasons. After all, knowing the laws of prosperity means we understand that we cannot give without receiving. How do we avoid a selfish intent behind our giving, such as having no strings attached?

A: This is a common challenge initially, but our concern disappears over time as our giving becomes more automatic than deliberate. Part of the answer you seek is that expecting the laws of prosperity to work is not selfish. How many people think selfishly about gravity working in their favor more than it does for others? Why not? Because we trust the equality of the laws of physics more easily than we trust the laws of prosperity.

Q: Why is that?

A: The laws of physics are grounded in the physical realm, so they work the same way for everyone on earth, whether we believe in them or not. The laws of prosperity require our mental acceptance and sharing accordingly if we want to be prosperous. That is the nature of all higher laws, such as love, grace, and prosperity.

Q: Higher laws remain relevant regarding how we live as souls when not in a human form. I can see that laws such as gravity and inertia mean little to us if we have no physical body.

A: Well said!

Q: So understanding "higher laws" is kind of like discerning the usefulness of a chessboard and pieces lying before us. They can be objects of little interest to us or open up a whole new world of entertainment and enjoyment if we choose to learn and play by the rules. Is that correct?

A: That metaphor points in the right direction for open and seeking people. Not everyone wants to learn to play chess, but everyone alive ultimately prefers the happiness of having balance in our health, wealth, and relationships.

Q: I've heard of problems that often occur when a couple has financial challenges and only one wants to tithe. What's to be done in that case?

A: The partner who desires to start tithing might negotiate only on the money they earn. If they can give from joy and without fear, the other partner will eventually see the benefits. The results will show that the increased prosperity came from their faith in tithing. Many partners of those who tithe learn to give joyously using this process as the guide.

Q: When developing a prosperity plan, are there limitations to consider beyond following the laws of prosperity?

A: Yes. Setting our course through prayer and meditation is a good start, but we must be open to how such prayers and planning are answered. If we insist on telling our Father how we should become prosperous, we can actually close ourselves off to the help we request.

Q: And what would be an example of that?

A: Say you have a business and desire to prosper. You logically set the goal of increasing sales to increase your wealth. You focus all your prayers and energies on accomplishing that goal. Perhaps the truth is that your greater spiritual growth would come from doing something else altogether. You might draw someone to you who would buy the business and free you to move on, except that this new prosperous path doesn't agree with your plan. Always maintain the mindset of asking for "this or better" rather than "do it this way" when it comes to achieving prosperity and being open to a better way our Father might offer.

Q: I see the value in being so flexible with our planning. And you're sure we can't be flexible by giving more of our time if we are uncomfortable donating as much as a tenth of our income?

A: We tend to receive in the form that we give. If we desire to give more of our time, we will receive the same from others. We can also use our skills and connections to help out where we're spiritually fed, resulting in receiving specialized help in our lives rather than directly increasing our wealth.

Q: I remember from the Bible that, "Not one jot or tittle will pass unnoticed until all is fulfilled." I guess that also applies to our choices regarding prosperity.

A: Perhaps a better way of phrasing that idea would be, "Don't spend time looking for loopholes when we could be pursuing the fullness of the love and wisdom we came here to attain."

Q: Any further advice to help attain prosperity in our lives?

A: Be as sure of our Father's desire for all His children to be prosperous as we are that the sun will rise and we will have air to breathe. Few spend any time fearing a lack of sun and air, but how quickly would we die without them? Our Father always provides exactly what we are ready for regarding our next steps on the path. Knowing that our loving Father is always with us assures our success.

Business Partners In Discord

One of my first self-employment ventures was with Eric. We were friends with a shared interest in being entrepreneurs as well as being skilled in radio broadcasting. We formed a partnership with my business knowledge and his recording studio equipment. We produced radio commercials for a living, and our success in that business was immediate.

We were quite happy working for ourselves and making good money as measured by two young business owners. However, Eric wasn't feeling fulfilled. His interest in the recording studio business was secondary to his desire to be an entertainer. He convinced me to expand our partnership by investing in a no-alcohol nightclub for teenagers. Eric wanted to run that business and leave the recording studio to me, though we'd be equal partners in both ventures.

To make a long story short, I agreed to his request, and we became joint owners of this second business less than three years after starting the first. I had to admit the recording studio was not as exciting a business as the teen nightclub turned out to be. I willingly worked weekends at the club to be a part of the excitement. This was in 1981, which happened to be the same year that the cable channel MTV first began to air music videos and related programming 24/7/365.

In early 1983, I went to Eric with a proposal to bring music videos to our club. The idea was to feature a giant screen TV playing the latest music videos. I also proposed a video camera showing our own dancers live on the big screen when the videos weren't playing. The amount needed to do all that was close to $20,000. His response and reasons for objecting to this idea changed everything.

It turned out that Eric and I disagreed on a basic premise of business. He felt the better way to make money was to save money. I was on the other side of that coin, feeling the better way to make money was by spending money to put your business ahead of the competition. Eric pointed out that there was no competition because we were the only teen nightclub in the county. I was convinced our greater success depended on constantly improving our "product." Doing anything less implied a lukewarm attitude toward our customers and business.

That was the beginning of the end of what had been a successful, albeit largely untested, partnership. I never regretted the split because our opposing perspectives toward money and improving the business were so different that going our separate ways was just a matter of time. While the split initially left hard feelings between us, Eric and I later reconciled and remain friends to this day.

That was just the first of many lessons I would learn about people and management in the years ahead.

Business

Q: A common cliché used to describe conflicts in our work is, "That's just business." That statement implies that we are expected to see and handle business matters differently than the non-business aspects of our lives. Is this dualistic approach correct?

A: Only if both "approaches" use love as the guide, but business matters are often not conducted that way. From a spiritual perspective, there should be no difference in how we treat our customers, co-workers, suppliers, or friends and family.

Q: While that makes a great deal of sense, why doesn't it come more naturally to us to treat all the people we encounter in those different relationships the same?

A: This is often due to our earthly perspective and occurs when we don't see everyone as the unconditionally loved children of our Father. Once that separation occurs in our minds, then our natural reaction is to place people into a self-made caste system. That leads to a "dualistic approach" in treating and relating to others.

Q: But many business adages I grew up with seem like good advice. For instance, "Don't bring your personal problems to work." Shouldn't there be a separation between our personal challenges and those we have in business?

A: Yes, in terms of not allowing the tough challenges in one area of our lives to negatively affect how we treat others. But that applies to any aspect of our lives, not just home and business.

Q: How about something more specific like, "Don't date your co-workers"?

A: In a perfect world, there is nothing wrong with personal relationships among co-workers. In this imperfect world, dating co-workers adds an additional challenge to the relationship and workplace. In truth, if the relationship went well, as they sometimes do, the two people would be a great couple and excellent co-workers. More often, however, conflicts between them cause both situations to become untenable.

Q: So, is the adage of not dating co-workers based on the likelihood of a poor outcome, statistically speaking, rather than being a blanket rule that no one should break?

A: Correct. There is little difference between not dating co-workers and why people avoid friendships between supervisors and subordinates. If the friendship sours, it is difficult to maintain a good working relationship. One person often believes the other is taking advantage of their friendship.

Q: What is the best management style that would allow us to maintain a spiritual perspective when making business decisions? This is especially tricky in today's litigious society.

A: You have just touched on a significant spiritual dilemma we all face. There is always the law to follow, but there is also the loving manner in which Jesus taught us to treat each other.

Q: Exactly! Those two approaches often seem at odds with each other. How do we know the correct way to proceed in a particular situation?

A: As long as we don't see a "win/win outcome" for all those involved in the choices we consider, following the law and acting as Jesus taught will often seem at odds to us. Starting from the perspective that we are all siblings in God's beloved family helps us to see why both the lawful and loving approaches are never at odds.

Q: But let's say a person borrows money and does not pay it back according to the terms of the agreement. Do we ignore the debt out of compassion, or do we take action to collect what's owed?

A: You have had both situations occur to you and have made different choices regarding how to proceed. Why did you forgive the debt in some cases, and in others, you made efforts to collect?

Q: In the cases where the debt was forgiven, I felt that I was not harmed and that they were simply unable to repay me rather than unwilling or negligent. When I felt the person who owed money to me was trying to avoid paying me back, or their own selfish choices made them unable to pay me back, I felt making efforts to collect was appropriate.

A: Just so. It all comes down to a case-by-case basis, where we pray and meditate on the situation to determine which would be best. Another adage that works well in lending money to friends or family is "Don't do it if you will feel cheated if they don't pay you back."

Q: Why is that? Are friends and family members less trustworthy than others in the world?

A: Not at all. There are, however, conflicting expectations on both sides of such loans. The lender often feels that a friend or family member should feel more beholden to repay a loan. The borrower often feels the friend/family member/lender should understand their situation more and not pursue payment until they can easily repay what's owed.

Q: Let's move on to management styles in business. Doesn't it make sense that we would relate differently to people in business than we do on a personal basis?

A: Yes and no. We should always treat or manage others with love and respect. That does not mean tolerating less than an acceptable effort and outcome from a subordinate or even a customer. We may choose to handle the same kind of situation differently with a family member.

Q: So, would Jesus fire a poor worker rather than give them as many chances as needed to perform up to standards?

A: Absolutely, but then Jesus would know exactly what was needed to draw the best out of each person. If, after all reasonable efforts, the person and job were not a good fit, Jesus would indeed let them go. However, Jesus would also know of a better career path for them and even help them obtain that job. It is not advisable to think we are doing someone a favor by keeping them in a job where they don't thrive and perform well.

Q: Most managers would say that watching out for the personal welfare of an employee is not their responsibility. At what point should we draw the line in helping others, especially in the business world where "time is money?"

A: That is where most go astray in their thinking, and the litigious trend in society today adds to this. Managers also believe that efforts made toward helping a troubled employee take time away from pursuing the company's profit goals. However, the bigger picture shows us that the goals of the company and helping its staff members are all compatible when love is the guide.

Q: Could you explain that in more detail?

A: Gladly, this concept is sadly missing in most organizations. Many people believe that leaders in any industry are in those top positions because they have developed and executed the best business strategy. If all other factors are the same, this indeed would be true. But it does not matter if the goal is higher profits, a more extensive client base, an expanded facility, a greater market share, or achieving any other competitive advantage; the law of love trumps them all.

Q: And an example would be…?

A: The employee who was not a good fit makes this point quite well. Taking the time to find a better match for their talents and what brings them joy does not take away from the company achieving its own goals. The universal laws reward such loving behavior by attracting greater abundance to all firms operating in harmony with our Father's loving ways. This is not to say that we can slack off in running the business, but making an extra effort to help another soul get on the right career path aligns with what we are on the earth to learn. Applying our Father's loving business ways should be part of every strategic plan.

Q: You mentioned that our litigious society affects our business decisions. Shouldn't we be concerned with the legal ramifications of HR activities?

A: Yes, but not in a fearful way. We should render unto Caesar as the law requires. We are divinely protected when we make our choices out of love rather than fear. Jesus purposefully avoided many conflicts during His ministry until it suited Him and His strategic plan to submit to the Roman legal system. This is not to say we will never become entangled in legal proceedings, but if we handle them as Jesus did, the outcome will always be for the best.

Q: So you're saying that our combined thoughts and efforts act like a magnet to attract or repel the prosperous conditions and/or the tough challenges we encounter? Of course, that is how individual karma works, but how does that work for the overall business?

A: The more harmonious a business is, the more it is run with the law of love, and the more prosperous it will be if it follows good business practices. Shoppers will be naturally attracted to buy the goods such companies sell because of the loving vibrations instilled in each of their products. Even the highest quality products will not be successful in the long run if the firm selling them does not seek a win/win result in their choices.

Q: What about businesses that are run poorly or selfishly and still succeed for some time?

A: This happens often, but to what end? Organized crime continues because of their short-term successes, but that kind of achievement is full of fear for all involved. Even churches run by selfish motives can seemingly succeed for a time, but they will ultimately fail. Nothing out of harmony with the will of our Father is everlasting.

Q: That leads me to the question of competition. Should we not have companies competing against each other? There is an implication in what you are suggesting that sounds like a free market economy compares poorly to something like a communistic approach.

A: That is neither true nor the point. Competition is good as long as it is done in the spirit of encouraging everyone to excel in what they do while the customer and economy continue to benefit. If one competitor employs unloving or unethical tactics to gain an advantage, the result will not be sustainable success.

Q: Why hasn't the communistic approach been more financially successful than the free market economy?

A: Neither is better than the other. It is a matter of which approach is more harmonious with the mindset of the citizens it governs. A free market economy allows greater freedom of choice for this country's citizens despite the inherent drawbacks that led to times like the Great Depression. When there is greater trust and equality in education, and the citizens agree that we are all part of the same spiritual family, almost any approach to an economy will prosper.

Q: Is socialism any better than either of those systems?

A: Different? Yes. Better? No. The same weaknesses in us as individuals become the "weakest link" that hinders the progress of any approach to government and economics. That is why the best way to turn any challenging situation around is to start making the desired changes from within.

Q: That brings me back to leadership and management styles. Is there one way to lead and manage people that is better than others?

A: Yes. Jesus was the perfect role model for this.

Q: I have often thought of Jesus as a great leader, but thinking of Him as a manager of others is new to me. Can you elaborate on that?

A: There was much more to Jesus' work than walking around the Holy Land and giving impromptu sermons. There were many followers of Jesus, and so was the network of people involved in His ministry. To understand this better, you have only to observe what it takes to produce a simple Sunday morning church service. Jesus was an excellent manager of people. He always knew how to draw the best out of them.

Q: Well, being able to foresee the outcome of all the choices He had before Him must have made that easier. What do you mean by saying Jesus could always draw the best out of His followers?

A: He always lived according to what He taught. There was no job beneath Him, and He equally honored all the efforts made. He trusted His followers to carry out what needed to be done. He inspired them so well that inspecting their work was rarely required. Jesus found coercion or discipline unnecessary. Knowing everyone was doing the right job and doing the best they could, His role as "leader" was mainly one of encouragement and guidance. Ensuring the right people were in the right jobs was the key to making this possible.

Q: And what about those of us who are not God incarnate? Can we expect that using the same leadership and management techniques as Jesus would work just as well for us?

A: You are correct in knowing that Jesus had much more going for Him as a leader and manager than most souls on earth. However, that is no reason to employ fear and/or "Do as I say, not as I do" as our preferred management style. We will all make mistakes on our Prodigal path back to our Father. Still, we should always try to be loving, encouraging, honoring, and trusting regarding how we treat others, management included.

Q: When you say "fear," I assume you mean to motivate your employees to perform at an acceptable level, knowing that if they do otherwise, it will result in fewer promotions, raises, and even discipline or termination.

A: There's far more to invoking "fear" as a manager or leader than what you just said, but your statement captures the point quite well.

Q: But what of the employees who respond better to what I'll call "fearsome management techniques?"

A: There are few such people. A fearsome management style may appear to succeed at times. However, those with the skills needed to do the job will respond better to their supervisors' love, trust, and encouragement.

Q: And what happens if it is not a goal of management to have a happy staff that desires to remain with the organization?

A: Using other management styles, even employing fear, does not mean automatic failure for the business, but they will not be as successful, and their employee turnover will undoubtedly be higher. If the leadership does not have a win/win strategy that includes a contented staff among their goals, the organization can still limp along if they are of service in other areas.

Q: I also noticed your caveat of employees "who have the skills you need." What does that mean or imply?

A: Hiring the wrong person for a job is entirely possible. Their skills and joy in life may be a better fit in a different position, and that job may well be with another company. The lesson here is to hire the right person for each job the first time. It goes along with the old cliché "measure twice, so you cut only once." This, again, goes back to using our intuition, prayer, and meditation to make better choices.

Q: So managers sometimes hire the wrong person to do a job? Can this be overcome through customized testing and better interview techniques?

A: That would help, but those improvements would not offer the best results for the effort expended. Using our intuition, prayer, and meditation in choosing the right person for each job will result in greater success than other HR techniques we might use. Aligning our will with the loving ways of our Father while we ask for guidance in our work is our most powerful management tool.

Q: Why are intuition, prayer, and meditation better than all the "best practices" businesses use today when hiring the right people?

A: Because using such gifts to everyone's advantage is what we're here to learn. Successfully managing a profitable business, even if it is of great service to others, is secondary to each of us becoming a better person. What does it profit anyone to gain the world if they lose their soul in the process? Jesus could not have stressed enough that when we seek the kingdom of heaven first, all other things are given to us.

Q: Why does the cliché, "I'd rather be lucky than good," come to mind here?

A: That is an amusing description of the expected outcome when we make loving, win/win choices ahead of all else. Suddenly, "luck" seems to come our way in the helpful people and timely breaks we attract into our lives. The truth is that luck is better defined as 99% karma and 1% chance. Those who understand this concept know that "being good brings good luck."

Q: Our top CEOs should spend their days praying and meditating rather than studying and planning their business strategies. Is that really the case?

A: If someone insists on being out of balance, perhaps that is the better extreme. But the answer to your question is "no." Extreme attitudes and actions do not offer sustainable win/win outcomes that cultivate love and happiness in our lives. One of the great tenets of Buddhism is achieving balance in all things. Too much of any particular behavior can disrupt our plans, even if that "imbalance" favors a spiritual extreme over a physical one.

Q: Why do we tend to favor an unbalanced approach? If achieving balance in all things is the natural way of all creation, what makes this so difficult for us?

A: That is counted among the best questions you could ask. The answer is that we tend to go in the direction of our strengths and desires. Remember the counsel your human father used to offer, "When the only tool you have is a hammer, everything looks like a nail." Many managers and leaders feel more comfortable strategizing and coercing than encouraging and listening to the divine within. That preference is why we willingly step onto the slippery slope and seek the extreme solution using our preferred strengths over a loving, balanced approach.

Q: And what about managing people in particular? Does this concept work the same way?

A: Yes. Jesus' management style will always succeed, but it also requires the greatest effort out of us as individuals and leaders. Consistently setting an example, loving and respecting others, and seeing how we can best serve their needs in achieving the company goals is rarely the preferred management style of most people. We become very good at getting things done by imparting orders and invoking fear than we do in drawing the best out of others. Cooperation should not be defined as everyone doing only what their manager tells them to do or else.

Q: So why do many people prefer to micromanage others, use fear to motivate, and generally "get in our way"?

A: That is certainly not the intention of most who manage that way. Their style emerges from wanting to help. They feel they are in management positions because they have been called to make a difference. That part is true. But over-managing, as you just described, occurs through a desire to be seen as the one who made it happen. If they draw the best out of others so that each one succeeds, the manager may fear that they won't be recognized as the catalyst for the overall success. To that end, over-managing serves two purposes. First, it keeps everyone's focus on the manager. Second, the manager in question is then certain their "unique leadership style" was the essential ingredient for the success of all.

Q: We can easily get in our own way without knowing it. That brings to mind another cliché. It's been said that having "all power is all corrupting." Is that true?

A: Since our Father is all-powerful, you know that it is not. But having access to more power than we know how to use correctly often goes awry. That is why the universal laws maintain our access to power at a level we can handle. We are automatically restricted in the mischief we can cause until we again learn to "play well with others." Those who don't choose love as their guide tend to make more "noticeable" mistakes when given greater power.

Q: Most managers don't see themselves as out of balance, even if their staff and even family members would disagree. How do we recognize when we're not following the perfect management example of Jesus?

A: You are correct that most do not realize it when managing through fear rather than love. We can ask ourselves if we've ever thought or said, "They had better measure up. Don't they know how many people would love to have their job?" If we have felt this way, then a different approach is recommended. Also, if a co-worker asks why a decision was made and the response is, "Because I'm in charge," then fear and control are their preferred "hammer" in getting the most out of their staff.

Q: But isn't that why a leader is in charge of making the final decision?

A: Of course, but to do so by leaving others questioning the "why" behind those orders does not bring out the best in them. Many leaders say they prefer a transparent leadership style but honestly do not. Such leaders find it easy to list reasons why transparency is inappropriate "in this particular case." A leader making decisions from love, like Jesus, would not hesitate to offer the sound reasoning behind any of their thoughts, even for decisions not yet finalized.

Q: But what does a staff member do when they disagree with the decisions?

A: That is also a great time to use intuition, prayer, and meditation. Cooperation and patience will often see us through until an agreed-upon solution is reached. When our best efforts don't resolve fundamental conflicts, then perhaps it is time to move on, not out of fear or anger, but because even the best intentions can turn bad when there is constant disagreement.

Q: Would this guidance be any different regarding non-profit or religious organizations?

A: No. The values the co-workers likely share that drew them together in the first place should make a loving and transparent management style easier to accomplish.

Q: While that makes sense, major conflicts still occur in altruistic organizations. How can that be avoided?

A: From where most people are now, whether working in for-profit or non-profit organizations, conflict is often inevitable. Having many ideas and everyone sharing a common ideal is best. When co-workers' shared ideal becomes convoluted, our "many ideas" become a hindrance rather than a help. Returning to a shared ideal once dissension becomes common requires patience, cooperation, and trust in the organization's leadership.

Q: That scenario applies to divorce, reorganizations, bankruptcies, and even world wars.

A: Very true. In business, the focus is most often on profitability and efficiency. Profits would grow even more if we encouraged all concerned to get behind a loving ideal in setting and achieving the company's goals.

Q: Any last words of advice or encouragement regarding how we should conduct business?

A: Jesus is the perfect pattern to follow, though many feel He was not a businessman. One's ability to make good management appear effortless is often the better measurement of competence. The fearful manager who wants to follow in the gentle steps of the Master may worry they will not appear to be needed. However, the manager who selflessly follows Jesus' path can't help but be noticed, admired, and valued. If we can keep this in mind, then our ego remains in check as we "fearlessly" draw the best out of ourselves and others.

Sigmund

My mother had a precious sheltie dog named Sigmund. Stephanie and I love dogs and were constantly taking Sigmund for a walk around the block where my mother lived. Sigmund, too, loved this tradition, and the neighbors were used to seeing the three of us make our rounds.

One neighbor on our route also had a sheltie. Her dog was a girl and was much smaller than Sigmund. One day, the neighbor asked if Sigmund had ever been neutered. I told her no, but since he was my mother's only dog, unwanted puppies were not an issue. The neighbor said she was asking for a different reason.

It seems both Sigmund and her sheltie were AKC certified, and the neighbor wanted to breed them to sell the offspring for profit. She said it was typical for the male owner to get the pick of the litter if they preferred. I told her I had no problem with that, but that Sigmund was my mother's dog, and I would ask if she was okay with this.

My mother said she had no interest in breeding dogs, but she also didn't mind if the neighbor wanted to do that. With my mother's consent, we all agreed to bring Sigmund to the neighbor's house the next day.

When we arrived, the neighbor invited us to bring Sigmund into her backyard. She brought out her sheltie, Tiffany, and we allowed them to introduce themselves. Sigmund was immediately interested in Tiffany, but neither of them had any experience with this sort of thing. Ultimately, they never were able to let nature take its course and produce a litter.

In retrospect, I looked at the morality of all that had transpired. Had society applied the laws of humans to how we treat canines, we should have been arrested. From that perspective, there was pandering, profit, and potential slavery behind what occurred with Sigmund and Tiffany. If they were our children instead of our pets, we would have been labeled among the worst criminals in the world.

I introduce the next chapter with that broader perspective regarding where we draw the line on sexual morality.

Sexual Morality

Q: It has been said that an ongoing challenge for humankind is creating a spiritual balance for our sexual urges. How do we balance our sexual desires so that they are in accord with God's will?

A: Sexual urges were created to ensure procreation, but there are also mental and spiritual aspects to sex that go well beyond the physical. The spiritualization of our sexual urges means balancing the physical, mental, and spiritual facets of sex with love as the guide.

Q: Could you give an example of perfectly balanced sexual urges between, say, a typical married couple?

A: First, sex does not require the intent of procreation to be in balance. It is a beautiful way to express love for another person with or without desiring a larger family. So, on the physical level, sexual urges are better satisfied in ways that also express love. On the mental level, choosing a sex partner you are in love with helps maintain balance. On a spiritual level, a sexual experience is felt more as a sharing in the Oneness of all life. While that may not sound very exciting to us on earth, the ecstasy experienced at the soul level far surpasses that of an orgasm in the physical.

Q: Does that mean "coupling" can occur without a physical body?

A: Yes, but think of souls choosing to synchronize their vibrations rather than a physical coupling. In the same way that resonant frequencies cause tuning forks to vibrate even though they are not touching, the loving alignment of the souls' vibratory patterns also opens their minds to each other. The intense love and joy shared during this alignment is indescribable in human terms.

Q: So is it wrong to enjoy sex when we are not in love and/or have no intention of making a life together with the other person?

A: This is always a personal choice of right or wrong. In truth, we are all lovable and will be together forever. So, the question we need to ask ourselves about our sex partners is why we're choosing to be with them. Are we manifesting our love through sex, or are we simply satisfying our carnal desires?

It may help to think of sex like a prayer. Do we desire to commune with our Father lovingly or selfishly pray to get what we want? Having sex with selfish intent is not the horrible sin many believe it to be. But like so many other selfish choices, sex without love is a slippery slope that can be addictive. Unlike illegal drugs, the adverse effects of sex with selfish intent are not so easily seen even after we're hooked.

Q: I don't mean to be crude, but what about masturbation? Is there such a thing as that when there is no physical body?

A: Yes, but the full answer offers a very different perspective than you have now. In the case of masturbation, with whom do we align if not with another soul? While a human typically sees masturbation as a solo act, the soul understands that we are never alone. Our Father is always with us, and communicating perfectly with Him is our highest natural state. So, there is no such thing as being alone when we open our minds to His presence.

Q: While that's great to know, it will take some getting used to thinking of all our intimate moments being shared with God. Somehow, I don't think I'm alone in imagining God looks the other way while we're sexually involved.

A: Not opening our hearts, minds, and souls to our Father's loving ways when involved in sex is one way we become out of balance. Sex without love, love being another name for our Father, can take us down a different path from the one back Home.

Q: I'm not sure I follow you there. What happens if we aren't inviting God into our bedrooms, so to speak?

A: In the same way that a pebble dropped into water spreads ripples, every choice we make and action we take causes vibratory ripples in the universe. We don't realize as humans that those vibrations seek balance. Every choice we make in harmony with love is always in balance, for that is the pure nature of all perfect things. Every choice made with selfish intent requires balancing, which automatically invokes the law of karma, meaning we will reap the selfishness we've sown. Karma ensures that we reap what we sow with loving choices as well, but then there is no suffering.

Q: I understand the concept of "an eye for an eye," but I'm lost on how "balance" manifests if we have a selfish intent behind our sexual acts.

A: The various manifestations of sexual karma are nearly infinite. In some ways, it would be easier for humans to understand if we contracted a severe STD every time we made a poor sexual choice. But karma is meant to be instructive rather than a punishment, so instead, we reap only what we sow. However slowly it happens, our selfish sexual desires can and do become addictive. Most people understand how difficult addictions are to overcome, but by the time we realize the habit we've built with our selfish choices, the addictive craving is entrenched.

Q: So an addiction to, say, prostitutes or pornography or some deviant form of sex started with a selfish motivation for sexual gratification without love being involved?

A: That is often the case. If we never made a selfish choice regarding sex, how could we end up addicted to the things you just mentioned?

Q: So, how do you define deviant sex? Is that reserved for pedophiles and the like?

A: Since all deviant sex starts with a desire that excludes love, the strict definition is self-evident. Most often, it is a matter of individual choice when drawing the line to classify a given sexual practice as "deviant."

Q: So, is having sex with the same gender considered deviant sex?

A: You haven't asked that question in a proper context. A better answer can be given if asked in this way, "Is love the motivation behind this particular sexual activity?" The gender of the people involved has no moral consequences.

Q: A strong argument I've heard against homosexuality is that the human body was developed for a man and woman to procreate. What does one say to people who believe homosexuality itself is a sin, especially given the warnings against it in the Bible?

A: Those same people might ask if Jesus was going against our Father's design for humanity when He chose to be celibate. For most people, abstaining from sex their whole lives creates a different kind of challenge in remaining balanced. For Jesus, it was simply the right choice.

Q: How does Jesus' choice of abstinence relate to my question regarding the morality of homosexuality?

A: It still comes down to the individual's intent behind their sexual choices. It is confusing to have the majority vote on which sex acts should be considered immoral while others are socially acceptable. Cheating on a spouse has been acceptable behavior and shunned by society, which has changed back and forth over many centuries and circumstances. It is better to start with the most loving way to manifest our preferred sexual desires and then choose which activities best support that path. Regardless of what we decide is right for us, we should never condemn the choices of others.

Q: But how does a homosexual desire begin if procreation was the original intent behind creating two genders? Perhaps you can give an example?

A: An example will help to understand this controversial issue better. Since souls have no gender, you might say we are all the same gender. In that light, every sex act is a homosexual one when souls physically couple. This is a human perspective and not shared by those in higher planes, but it helps to remove the stigma of having sex with the same gender.

Given that genderless perspective regarding sex and our souls, let's deal with the real question. Does homosexuality always have selfish roots in how it begins? The answer is no.

For example, what if a soul has consistently been reincarnated as a woman and then has an opportunity to return to a man, which will offer them better opportunities for spiritual growth? Given that their sexual preference for men had been well established over many heterosexual female lifetimes, their sexual orientation would not necessarily switch because of the change in human gender.

Q: I can follow that, but can't a person's sexual orientation be programmed in the body's DNA according to what would serve the greater purpose in their next human life?

A: Our DNA is "programmed" according to our past choices. Nothing in the universe is stronger than our free will, especially when reinforced through our choices made over many lifetimes. An orientation toward heterosexuality is not required for greater spiritual growth. What if the person who would best support your spiritual progress in this lifetime is the same gender? Add to that the possibility that key people who would be of the greatest spiritual support in your life are also part of the homosexual community. Then, it would make sense to have both partners homosexually oriented regardless of gender.

Q: But what of society's bias against such couples? Isn't that taking on a difficult life that isn't karmicly due to them?

A: Perhaps, but learning not to discriminate against others for any reason can also be learned this way. Even with no negative karma involved, one or both of the partners can choose (rather than be naturally drawn) to incarnate with a homosexual orientation to be a role model for their friends and family, showing how to live such a socially controversial lifestyle in a very loving way.

Q: That sounds like homosexuality is a choice rather than being born that way. Is that correct?

A: The better answer is that it is both. We can be naturally drawn to a homosexual preference through DNA or patterns developed in our past lives. We can choose to be homosexual in a lifetime to enhance our greater spiritual growth or help others to do the same. We can even find ourselves attracted to a person of the same gender today because of the past relationships we've had with them, even though we are presently wired to be heterosexual. Each soul's mind remembers all our past relationships, and we consciously react accordingly. Believing in reincarnation makes understanding this much easier. The stigmas people maintain regarding being born homosexual versus choosing to be homosexual become moot when all the combinations involving reincarnation are considered.

Q: But what of the homosexuals who don't set a loving example for everyone else?

A: Sexuality makes no difference in this. We must always overcome our past selfish choices. If we are addicted to sexual behaviors that are not based on love, there are consequences to experience and lessons to be learned. This concept applies no matter what our sexual orientation might be.

Q: I think I get it now. Having a hetero or homosexual orientation is neither right nor wrong. It is our intention behind our sexual choices that indicates whether love or selfishness is our guide. Being born with a homosexual orientation does not by itself say we have made poor sexual choices in the past, and it doesn't matter. Either way, it is up to us to be motivated by love in our present sexual choices, no matter what we have done in the past.

A: Nicely said! Trying to "second guess ourselves" as to whether we are meeting negative karma due to our past choices or if we are freely choosing to be loving role models to others makes no difference. Regardless of the reason behind our current challenges, making the best choices we can from a foundation of love is always the perfect answer.

Q: So let me get into some specifics about sex other than homosexuality. What about sex before marriage?

A: Our Father created both sex and procreation. Although humans created the sacrament of marriage, committing to such a loving relationship is in keeping with His loving ways. Having sex as a married or unmarried couple is only "wrong" if the rules we morally set for ourselves say it is. As long as the intentions behind our sexual relations are loving, there is no sin involved. If humankind wants to make additional rules to live by that do not cause harm or condemn others, that is certainly allowed and is one of the infinite ways in which free will manifests on the earth.

Q: Is there an "age of consent" whereby all should abstain from sexual relations until they reach it?

A: Yes, but that is not a "fixed" chronological age. Because of the unique challenges that sexual issues present, it could be rightly said that we are rarely properly prepared to make such choices at any age. Setting the age limit after puberty is a given, and recognize in advance that wherever you set the age of consent, it will be a rule that is inevitably broken. The question you're about to ask about older individuals taking sexual advantage of younger people is a different issue. It becomes a question of criminal law when one takes undue advantage of another's lack of understanding. Such choices to take advantage of others will always be selfish and morally wrong.

Q: Why was being celibate something Jesus chose? Is that a rule He put on Himself, or did God require that of Him?

A: No rules stand in our way once we have obtained the Christ Consciousness. Jesus "became the law," meaning He makes only loving choices with each new opportunity. What law could stand in judgment of such choices? Jesus decided to remain celibate because not taking a partner in that lifetime best supported what He came to the earth to do.

Q: I'm not sure what you mean by that.

A: His life would be one of complete service to others. Jesus knew He would be traveling for most of His life, spending a great deal of time studying and presenting a new worldview. Even after Jesus assumed His role as Teacher, He knew the time needed to raise a family properly was not a good fit with all He had committed to do. Finally, knowing that He would likely not live past 33, Jesus would have been challenged to be a good father and support a family. As you can see, His choice to remain celibate was just a part of the life and purpose Jesus came in to fulfill.

Q: But wasn't that difficult for Him? I mean, Jesus was human with a human body and carnal desires like all the rest of us, wasn't He?

A: Not exactly. Experiencing the carnal appetites of the human body, once our minds have been perfected, is not as compelling as it is to someone enmeshed in the earth. Think of an addict's desire for their drug of choice compared to one who does not take drugs. An addict's thoughts always revolve around how to get high. The non-addict takes little notice of drugs or getting high even when the opportunity arises.

Q: But surely, as the world's most perfect man, thousands of people wanted to be "with" Jesus in every sense of the word. How did He deal with that?

A: Science has not yet learned to measure the vibrations we send to each other with our thoughts. It might help to think Jesus was controlling His body's production of sexual pheromones in making sure He exuded a loving but non-sexual vibration. Jesus always sent out a "platonic vibe," as you might call it today, so the automatic response from others was consistent with His intention.

Q: So you're saying that if we want to have sex with other people, all we have to do is set our minds to it, and they'll respond?

A: People will respond, although it may not be the people we had in mind. It will be those people who resonate with the vibratory pattern we're sending. It becomes clear why loving intent is so important in this regard.

Q: What about the social taboos against incest? Are the prevailing laws against having sex with our family members a construct of human laws or common sense?

A: Both, actually. The taboos against incest make sense from both a genetic perspective and do not confuse a family's spiritual growth opportunities with sexual challenges among its members.

Q: But I assume Jesus has perfect genes, right? I mean, the whole genetics thing would not be a problem in Jesus' case, would it?

A: You are correct in saying those limitations do not apply to Jesus. But then, it is rarely correct for people to remain celibate even though that was His own perfect choice. There is a great difference between what Jesus would do in a given circumstance and what He would suggest for others, given their limited understanding of our Father's loving ways. Don't forget the example of the addict's desire for drugs compared to one who doesn't take drugs at all. Drug addicts will not be able to measure up to the better choices a non-addict would make.

Q: I just thought of a couple more questions about homosexuality. First, the topic of licensing gay marriage is quite controversial. Should the marriage of same-sex couples be legally sanctioned?

A: The argument against it is that doing so would dishonor the sanctity of married heterosexual couples creating families. Let me ask if you personally feel same-sex marriages dishonor your own marriage and family.

Q: No, but then I believe we are all beloved siblings of our Father. Homosexual partners should have the same rights and considerations as anyone else. A million years from now, I doubt sex or gender will be an issue for any of us, so why should it be today?

A: Can you imagine how many others are just as convinced of the opposite point of view? It helps to see this using an example that removes sex from the discussion. Let's talk for a moment about flag burning.

Q: Seriously? How can gay marriage and flag burning be related?

A: Do you support a constitutional amendment that would ban the burning of the nation's flag? I know you don't, but why?

Q: If we attach great penalties to burning our nation's flag, won't we also make that very act more attractive to those aggressively trying to make themselves heard? My patriotic feelings are unaffected by anyone burning a flag to make a point.

A: And so it should be for same-sex marriage. It does not matter what others think or do regarding the sanctity of the marriage vows. As long as we see them for the loving covenant they are, the rest doesn't matter. Are there people who would use this issue to promote their political agendas for or against homosexuals? The answer is yes. Do the secular laws governing humans change the fact that we are to love our Father and one another as ourselves? The answer there is no.

Q: That leads to my other question, but you've answered it. I was about to ask, "Should we join together in a political way to bring attention to tolerance regarding bigotry of all types?" Given what you said, what is the best way to dissolve all this hatred?

A: Each person should follow their inner guidance for the best course to take. Some will be drawn toward actively organizing a political answer to this challenge. Others will feel that it is better to quietly role model loving behavior and greater tolerance. Some are convinced that both flag burning and homosexuality are wrong and will do their best to see that society's laws will not condone them. All those opposing beliefs will evolve over time and with patience into one world view of unconditional love.

Q: Any closing words of guidance and encouragement on all we've covered?

A: There is no better way to discern the answers to our moral and ethical questions than through prayer and meditation. The best way to change the world is to role model the changes we desire in others in our own lives. As we lovingly apply what we already know, more will be given in wisdom and opportunities to make a difference.

Unfinished Business

My mother passed away on July 16, 2008, from acute Leukemia. That was less than five weeks after first learning she was ill. I remembered that Edgar Cayce and his oldest son, Hugh Lynn, had agreed upon a word or phrase that would be used to validate if any communications with Edgar after he died were real. Just days before my mother's passing, I asked if she would be willing to set up a "validation word" with me. She agreed.

I brought her paper, a pen, and an envelope and asked her to write the word out and seal it without letting anyone see it. It took some effort for her to do this; she was so frail by now, but she seemed as interested in setting up this "experiment" as I was.

After her passing, the number 8 often came to my attention. Sometimes, I would randomly check the time at precisely 8:00, or the number would constantly appear as I dealt with being the executor of her estate. I saw the number 8 as her way of letting me know she was alive and well and checking in with me from the other side.

The envelope with the word she had written was filed away and forgotten for months. I had been busy with life, completing my graduate degree after retiring from full-time employment a few years before. I wondered if anything would catch my attention enough to bring me out of retirement. In March 2009, something finally did interest me.

I was attending the Sunday service at my church when the minister mentioned that their search for an Executive Director was still going on after nine months. I read the weekly program and saw an article describing this need in greater detail. I realized the position was probably a good fit for my skills, but I had not paid much attention to this over the past months.

Suddenly, I clearly "heard" a voice in my mind say, "Compute the numerological value of Unity!" This is not something I normally do because I know little of what specific numbers are supposed to mean. I knew how to determine a word's numerological value and did as the thought suggested. I grabbed a pencil and calculated the numerical values of the word "unity." I should not have been surprised when it turned out to be an 8. I stood up right then, left the service, and picked up an application to apply for the job.

When I returned home with Stephanie, I told her what had happened and what I wanted to do. She was supportive and agreed I should apply. I then thought I should open the envelope to examine the word my mother left for me before she passed. I hesitated because there was nothing to verify regarding any message that might have come from my mother through someone else. Still, the thought persisted, and I went to get the envelope.

When I opened it, the word she had written for me was "business." She had misspelled it to read "busines" with only one "s." That was hardly like my mother, who was precise about such things. Then, I realized that I should compute the numerological value of the word "business." When I did, it came out to be the number 9. As I sat there trying to make sense of everything, I remembered that my mother had left the second "s" off the word she wrote. Since an "s" has a value of 1 in numerology, the word "busines," as she misspelled it, came out to an 8.

I put it all together. The number 8 was certainly her way of connecting with me from the other side, but she was also letting me know I had "unfinished business" to complete. That was what convinced me to apply for and accept the job at the Unity Church just 10 days later.

While mine is far from a scary story, it serves as an encouraging lead-in to the following chapter, *Things That Go Bump In The Night.*

Things That Go Bump in the Night

(Spirit Plane Communications)

Q: There is a great deal of confusion and fear regarding the supernatural, especially stories of things "not of this earth" that want to harm us. Are all ghost stories just made up, or is there really something to be afraid of from the other side?

A: There is never any reason to fear such things unless you give them the power to do so.

Q: And how do we empower such things?

A: First, by believing they can harm us. Second, holding on to feelings of fear and guilt opens a connection between believing we deserve to suffer and the forces willing to accommodate us. Third, we attract less-than-loving people from the other side when we participate in unsafe activities.

Q: Do "unsafe activities" include things like channeling and Ouija boards? If so, what effect do these risky methods have when opening doors to the other side?

A: Inviting beings from the "other side" to speak through us is a random process at best. It is not unlike doing interviews with people passing on the street. Many times, the beings have no selfish intent, and the "interview" is done with no ill effects. Other times, the being called has a selfish agenda and can end up as a stalker once having been introduced. Some don't have a selfish agenda but crave to be heard and admired as a great sage, whether they are or not. These, too, can end up following people around because both the incarnate and discarnate souls are looking to each other for their 15 minutes of fame.

Q: Just what kind of discarnate beings are we speaking of here? Are they always souls not currently in human form? Are they demons of some sort? What about stories of angels who have gone astray as followers of Lucifer?

A: Most often, the beings communicating in such a manner are souls. They can be angels, too, although we haven't been speaking of how to invite such enlightened help into our lives. To be clear, there are no evil angels. Lucifer is a confused soul like the rest of us. Lucifer became an archetype of selfishness because his story perfectly illustrates how a perfect soul can go astray. In truth, Lucifer, too, will eventually and freely come to accept our Father's loving ways as his own.

Q: I want to come back to those "better ways" to work with angels, but let's finish talking about the kind of souls who would not offer the highest guidance. How do we know a good spiritual source from a bad one?

A: How do you know the difference between good advice and bad advice? Through discernment. Does the information offered harm you or others? Does it appear and feel to be loving and ethical? Is the guidance consistent with the highest standards of what you believe? The answers to all these questions and prayerful discernment will help distinguish the wheat from the chaff every time.

Q: So what are the other ways to help attract the right sources from the "other side" when desiring the highest source of information?

A: Start with prayers for protection and ask that any source not intending to be of the greatest help and hope in answering depart and not return. Use meditation and inspirational writing to receive the answers to the questions of your heart. These differ from channeling, Ouija boards, and automatic writing because you are listening and then writing out what's given rather than actually allowing another entity to take control of your body. Higher sources rarely seek to take such control of humans. Any method of spirit plane communication that requires another entity to take control of your body can be problematic at best.

Q: So, does inspirational writing differ from automatic writing? In what way does it differ?

A: The former is done by listening in meditation and writing what you receive telepathically. Automatic writing and channeling are methods whereby another entity physically controls the body regarding what is communicated.

Q: Does a person doing inspirational writing hear an audible voice giving the information or guidance requested during meditation?

A: Hearing an audible voice can certainly happen, but most often, you will think the telepathic messages received are much like your own thoughts. With practice, your inspired answers will begin to offer information that you don't consciously already know.

Q: It seems that automatic writing and Ouija boards are a quicker and more verifiable way to know that the information is coming from the "other side" rather than wondering if we are writing things we're making up in our minds.

A: You just explained why the lesser method of gathering information from the "other side" is still so popular. It is easier to passively let others do the work than it is to properly attune ourselves to actively receive the highest possible guidance. The following analogy will help to understand the difference.

On Earth, it is much more difficult to find an expert to consult with on a specific subject than to ask people randomly passing by on the street, but which of those sources would we rather trust for the answers we seek?

Q: Point well taken. Why is it that what we see as the more difficult way to do something is often better?

A: This is a temporary perspective. There was a time before we became so enmeshed in the Earth that we favored what you referred to as the more difficult path. This includes the types of foods we eat, the exercises we use to balance the body, and loving our neighbor as we love God and ourselves. For example, think how uncomfortable an English teacher would feel using poor grammar when others find it easier to express themselves as they please. As we attain greater wisdom and patience, what we now see as the more difficult path will become the preferred path. Everyone will come to understand that the difficult path is the only one worth taking and that it is not demanding at all.

Q: Interesting! That seems similar to why a vegetarian does not find it difficult to maintain their diet even when bacon is frying, or a steak is cooking on the grill. Not eating meat is actually the preferred and even easier path for them.

A: Good analogy, except that we need not be vegetarians! Knowing the eventual goal of completely accepting our Father's loving ways helps us make better choices. Most find it comforting to know that we will eventually prefer what we now see as the more difficult path.

Q: So the better way is to start any spirit plane communications with a prayer for protection and then use meditation to open the door to the best guidance we can receive through inspirational writing. It may be a longer and more difficult way to obtain the desired results, but shortcut methods are often unreliable or even risky. Dare I ask what the worst-case scenario is when seeking unreliable guidance?

A: Some of the most selfish and misguided souls are drawn to controlling others this way. It is one thing to inflict suffering on others. It is even more attractive to such souls when they can get others to inflict suffering upon themselves. This is not said to scare anyone but rather to point out the logic in avoiding any spirit plane communication where we turn control of our body over to others.

Q: But I've heard good advice from people who channel spirit plane information. Is all that coming from lesser sources?

A: Not necessarily. Prayers of protection and the highest intention can and should keep all but the most enlightened spirit plane helpers away when the body is vulnerable. However, even the most gifted psychics can have a bad day when it comes to making the proper attunement.

Q: Probably one of the most famous psychics, Edgar Cayce, answered thousands of questions working with spirit plane communication. Was he subject to lesser entities trying to interfere with the highest guidance available?

A: Constantly, but few worked as hard as Edgar Cayce did to ensure such interference did not occur. Also, don't confuse what Edgar Cayce did with channeling. He most often spoke directly to the inquiring soul's higher self for medical information and went directly to the Akashic Records to answer the spiritual questions he was asked. To be sure, Edgar Cayce was divinely protected during the rare occasions when he channeled angels.

It is possible to work safely in this way, but starting with Ouija boards, channeling, or automatic writing is not advised, especially as the initial methods of spirit plane communication.

Q: Let's move on to people seeing ghosts and perhaps the activities of poltergeists. Are these kinds of stories made up, hallucinations, or did they actually happen to the people who tell them?

A: All three scenarios have occurred depending on the specific case. People do perpetrate hoaxes, while others have mental conditions that cause them to not see reality as most others do. There are also those things that occur where other realms and three dimensions cross paths, merging both realities for a time. Using a specific example will help to better answer your question.

Q: Let's start with the most common one, at least in the stories I've heard. That would be sightings of departed souls appearing as ghostly beings. What about examples where such sightings are part of our reality? How and why does this occur?

A: The soul is eternal, so the concept that the soul lives on after the death of the body is natural. Being able to see a soul who has crossed over to the other side can be attributed to a number of factors. The most common is that the soul has so enmeshed itself in the Earth that, after death, they do not choose to move on in their spiritual development. Even their vibrations are lower on the "other side" because of the lower consciousness they prefer. In most cases, the more earthly the consciousness of the "ghost," the easier it is for them to be seen in three dimensions. People on the Earth with a higher level of awareness of the infinite dimensions around them also have a greater ability to tune into the presence of such earthbound souls.

Q: So your use of the term "tune into" means that seeing "ghosts" from an earthly perspective is a function of both the departed soul having an earthly mindset in conjunction with the human's ability to see souls no longer in physical form?

A: Yes, you have the right idea, but some can also see higher vibration discarnate entities in three dimensions. It should be noted that this works the same in reverse. In order for people from the other side to communicate with those living on the Earth, they must be able to attune their communications to the appropriate vibratory level in three dimensions.

Q: You are speaking of telepathic communication, but I'm surprised to hear you speak of it in scientific terms. Can you expand on that?

A: Telepathy has a scientific foundation, like all spiritual concepts in three dimensions. Science will eventually learn to measure telepathic waves, which are not so different from the waveform communication now called radio broadcasting. The entire manifest universe operates according to scientific laws. Metaphysical things are only called such because human science has yet to understand how "supernatural events" lawfully work in three dimensions.

Q: If our soul's thoughts have physical vibrations, does that mean the soul has a physical body subject to physical laws?

A: It is easy to become confused here. The soul created in the image of our Father has no physical properties. Just as human babies are born naked, our Father created us in His perfect image of pure consciousness. In order to fully participate in the manifest dimensions, the soul assumes a physical form appropriate to where they are and what they are doing. On Earth, that form is a human body. Once we pass over to the other side, a less dense astral body is often more appropriate for the dimensions associated with our realm. The mind or brain of those "bodies" is what transmutes our thoughts into physical waves.

That is not to say that all telepathic communication requires a physical form to work. A different method of connection is used then, and the description exceeds current human and scientific understanding.

(Outer Darkness and Earthbound Souls)

Q: Is there any realm of existence that is denser than the Earth? I know that sounds like a pun, but I'm serious.

A: Yes, but you would not understand "denseness" the way you think of it here on Earth. For instance, when a soul has made truly dark choices and is so disruptive to others that they need to be sequestered for the good of all, they end up in a different dimension called Outer Darkness. This level of existence is so dense that nothing in that entire dimensional universe "moves." The soul remains in suspension or apart from all else without the ability to relocate or disrupt others.

Q: That sounds like the tortures of hell most religions say await the unfaithful. If nothing moves in Outer Darkness, how does a soul ever get away from there, assuming they can?

A: Our Father will always provide a way to escape every temptation. His unconditional love is eternal, as is His desire that every soul shares equally in all He has and is. A soul entrapped in Outer Darkness soon finds the only way out is to change their attitude by focusing on love as the guide. As long as their dark thoughts continue, their focus remains fixed on themselves, and the loneliness is nearly unbearable. Eventually, the suffering becomes so great they desperately cry out to our Father for help. Then, they realize they were never alone and that His loving light was always there, albeit ignored. It is only by dropping all pretenses and reaching out to our Father that they are able to receive the help they need.

Q: A dimension where everything is so dense that we can't move or interact? Our thoughts can become so selfish that we focus only on ourselves. That truly does sound like hell. But what of the souls entrapped on Earth? What happens that causes one soul to move on and another to remain on Earth even after the death of the body?

A: The only thing that holds them back is their awareness or lack thereof. Post-traumatic stress is as real on the other side as it is when we're in human form. After all, immobilizing trauma is in the mind, and the mind is eternal. When a soul becomes so traumatized by an event that they can't let go of it, they tend to relive the horrible event repeatedly in their minds. Even after the body dies, the soul can refuse to move on, preferring to remain in an endless loop of replaying the tragedy. This is a common "ghost story" of souls constantly reliving the events they cannot put behind them. Their lower vibrations can sometimes be perceived in three dimensions, especially in the early morning hours when humans have fewer distractions.

Q: What can be done for such unfortunate souls? Can we help them release from their tragic endless loop and the Earth?

A: Prayer on their behalf is always the best way. Beyond that, each case would be different. For instance, if the entrapped soul is forever repeating a similar pattern, it might be helpful if the earthly location where the trauma occurred was redecorated so it would be unfamiliar to them. The "new look" could serve to disrupt the soul's all-consuming focus on their traumatic experience. In that way, their attention could be redirected toward the guides and angels trying to help the soul move on with their life. Living "in the past" instead of "in the moment" is as much a challenge for us on the other side as it is here on Earth.

(Elementals)

Q: What about all of the folklore, including fairies, gnomes, gremlins, and all the rest? Are there places where such beings actually exist?

A: In Earth's three dimensions? No, except as noted, when occasionally, different realms can cross paths and merge for a time. The stories of such encounters are often based on those "crossings" and told by the people who were able to tune in and interact with the beings from those other realms. There are people who would lie about such things, too, but it is not hard to tell the difference between them.

Q: Are the beings of folklore always benevolent? I have heard stories that aren't always pleasant during such encounters.

A: This is a very difficult concept to explain so as to be understood in three dimensions. Some of the entities you mention can be souls from other dimensions and systems. They have free will and can choose to be loving or selfish in how they interact. Some are more like angels, and their choices are free if they do not harm. The toughest concept to explain is of those entities that are not truly alive but are actually animated thought forms. It might help to think of them as computer programs carrying out the purpose for which they were designed. So they can either aid or hinder others on the path as a free-willed entity programmed them to do so.

Q: Animated thought forms? Do they have a soul? If they are similar to a computer program, by what rules of etiquette should they be treated?

A: Those are interesting questions, though a bit off-topic. The quick answer is that they are not eternal, nor do they have souls, but that should make no difference in how we treat any creation. Treat them with the same regard as you would treat Jesus. That does not mean we should ever be less than "wise as serpents, yet harmless as doves" in protecting ourselves and our loved ones, but we lose little by being kind and respectful to all we meet.

Q: What about poltergeists? We hear stories of ghosts who seem to be able to do us harm. Is there any truth in that?

A: That depends upon the mindset of the intended victim. Such troubled souls on the "other side" are most often attracted to those on Earth who are easy targets. Being one who is more susceptible would include a belief in the poltergeist's ability to do them harm. Often, people who are addicted in some manner are less protected, and so they more easily attract such disruptive souls. If you ever find yourself around such a presence, then offer a quick prayer of protection. Reaffirm that if the entity is not there with the highest and best of intentions, then they must depart. Have faith in how well our prayers protect us, for our Father is always at our side.

Q: We have been speaking of those who don't inhabit physical bodies. However, some people I know claim we are under surveillance and occasional personal attacks from space aliens and even physical beings from other dimensions. Is there any truth to such claims?

A: It is a real challenge to answer you in a way that causes no fear. Let me say that there are numerous types of entities who would willingly disrupt our lives at any moment if given the chance. Everyone is protected in many ways from such interference, but some of those entities still manage to disrupt others to some degree. This is often because the intended victim karmically attracts disruptive forces to themselves, in effect overriding the automatic protections put in place. Be aware of physical and astral disruptive beings, and remember to protect yourself through daily prayer. Avoiding activities that create opportunities for them to interfere, such as Ouija boards, automatic writing, or addictive behaviors, is also wise.

Q: Some people, often those considered to be mentally ill, claim to be able to see into other dimensions. Is this an illness, or does it show their greater psychic abilities?

A: That depends on what they choose to do with what they see and experience, for while it can be a blessing, it is more often a hindrance. Does seeing into other dimensions help them become better, more loving people? If so, then that speaks for itself. More often, such experiences distract us from living in the moment.

Q: Any last helpful and hopeful words on this subject?

A: There is an obvious theme behind all we've discussed here. Some scary stories about encounters with beings that are "not of this world" have some basis. We place ourselves in harm's way by maintaining a less-than-loving attitude and/or practicing unsafe methods of spirit plane communication. Know that our Father is always with us, so what could stand against us? We need only keep our focus on Him and His loving ways to be protected.

From Conflict to Kumbaya

I was still 17 years old when I first began assessing our US political system. A good friend of mine was just barely of voting age and volunteered many hours on behalf of George McGovern's presidential campaign. I occasionally went with him and saw all the people working together with the goal of seeing their candidate elected. This was my first introduction to politics at a grassroots level, and I felt the store-front office was much like a church in how it drew people together who shared a common worldview.

It didn't take long for disappointment to set in. I was amazed that our political system often had potential candidates from the same party making near-slanderous statements about their opponents in an effort to win the primary election. Of course, McGovern prevailed through the primary system and went on to face Richard Nixon in the race for the presidency. The same negative rhetoric occurred repeatedly, except with more venom because of their fundamental platform differences. I was discouraged as I witnessed disparaging exchanges at every level of both campaigns, knowing how tough it would be to pull everyone together after the election was decided.

Nixon was ultimately elected and tasked with bringing the nation together in one accord. He was to accomplish that despite all the ugly accusations made by both sides during the national election campaign. Of course, that did not work, and not just because of the Watergate scandal.

I viewed our election system as fundamentally flawed. How could any system succeed that requires our political candidates to square off against each other and expect everyone to revere and support the one elected after the battle? I felt our political system was on par with "trying to pick up the chair in which you sit."

Having a spiritual perspective on life, even at that early age, I recognized that Jesus had not become the perfect role model for all time through politics. He showed us how to live a life of unconditional love and suggested that people follow Him if they found that His way of life and teachings appealed to them. Jesus was not elected to any position, yet it would be hard to find a better candidate to lead us toward accepting God's loving ways for our own.

It is easy to see why I don't believe politics is the answer when it comes to helping us become better people. I also don't see the world's various religions getting everyone to hold hands and sing Kumbaya. Despite believing that God is love, many religions unintentionally create divisions among us. This happens when their creeds teach that only their members are God's chosen people.

I have never understood why religions are so exclusive. The other kids on the block where I grew up were Mormon, Catholic, and Protestant. While I don't remember having theological discussions about our varying religious views, I do remember comments made by some of the parents regarding how wrong the "other religions" were. Such opinions came from believing that the "real truth" was taught only when they attended church.

I was raised to believe we would all eventually become perfect (enter heaven) regardless of our religious beliefs. To think that God would favor some of His children over others didn't make sense to me. After all, if God disliked someone enough to condemn them to eternal hell, why would He create them in the first place? I have matured and become more understanding of our political and religious differences since my early days, but the logic I've used to test such partisan beliefs has stayed with me. It is this perspective that guides my questions regarding religion and politics.

Religion, Politics & Science

Q: We are warned against mixing religion and politics, and yet here we are doing just that.

A: Conflict does not have to arise over this, but discussing either topic often polarizes people more quickly than most.

Q: The USA's founders and citizens decided that church and state (religion and politics) should remain separate. Why do both things often "bump heads" despite our desire not to mix them?

A: In this country, the function of most religions is to clarify how we should live by the tenets in their holy texts. The function of government is to enact written laws by majority vote that also dictate guidelines for our behavior. When they differ on moral issues, it is easy to see how religion and politics create conflicts.

Q: Is it better to side with our preferred religion when such conflicts arise?

A: You're implying that our chosen religion, if we have one, is a superior guide for how to live. That is not necessarily true. Both religion and politics are inventions of humankind and are double-edged swords in addressing the challenges they hope to resolve. Our loving Father's gentle ways would never work against His will like that.

Q: God didn't invent religion?

A: No. Religion, science, and politics are all inventions of humankind. They each seek to organize our view of existence and explain everything we once understood completely using only our intuition. Each of those studies has an area of strength the others lack, but truly understanding our loving Father takes far more than all three can offer, even when we try to combine them.

Q: So religion is all about God, but God doesn't focus on religion as the best way to become all we can be?

A: Correct. The Golden Rule and the Great Commandment are a better "focus" for us. Most religions are founded with the laudable purpose of living in harmony with each other and our Father's loving ways, but that changes over time.

Q: Why does that change?

A: Once the leadership of a religion feels it is their responsibility to "save souls," the expansion of their role is inevitable. What began as suggestions became rules, and those became "God's laws." The eternal penalty for breaking "God's laws" also became irreversible. Using fear to ensure compliance with the law is a compelling motive, but it will ultimately fail. As Jesus said, "Forgive them, Father, for they know not what they do."

Q: You're speaking of an eternal and irreversible hell for not following the traditional Christian creed?

A: Not exclusively, but that is one such case. When a creed is based on fear, many questions cannot be answered. The Bible says our loving Father does not want any soul to perish. Why, then, would He create laws with a time limit that work against His will so that every soul can be saved? If every soul is not saved, is our Father incapable of saving everyone or just unwilling? When would our perfect Father give up on any of His children? How could our loving Father be hateful, jealous, vengeful, or ever condemn His children? You get the idea from there.

Q: Does that mean politics and science have gone astray in the same way as religion?

A: Gone astray, yes, but not in the same way. Science seeks to uncover all the universe's secrets without including our loving Father as the First Cause or as part of the equation. Science seeks physical, repeatable proof of our Father's existence under its own terms without realizing their limited methods block a closer relationship with Him. If a scientist cannot prove our Father exists, which of them moved away from the other to cause such a separation? We Prodigal

Children will eventually return home because our Father did not force Himself on us.

Q: And where did politics go astray?

A: People misuse politics to legislate what is "optional" into required or coerced behavior by majority vote. Unfortunately, coercion of others, even by majority vote, rarely follows the loving ways of our Father.

Q: That was impressive! In just a few sentences, you've identified how to fix humanity's and the world's problems.

A: I may have identified the challenges before us in very basic terms, but can we briefly explore what "solutions" you see in what I just offered?

Q: Sure. We do the opposite of what you identified as the challenges before us. Religions should go back to "suggesting and supporting" the Golden Rule and the Great Commandment instead of dictating a specific way we should live. Science would do better to be open to God as the First Cause as they advance their research. Politics...well, you got me there. I don't know what they should do if politicians aren't voting in new laws and trying to get re-elected.

A: Actually, your last statement was the most revealing of all. Remember I said that religion, science, and politics were all inventions of humankind? The interesting and common reaction we all have is to use those three things as solutions or tools toward becoming better people, even when we know they are flawed and incomplete by design.

Q: But if we did away with churches, science endeavors, and government, the world would be in chaos, wouldn't it?

A: A humorous answer is appropriate here because this subject is daunting. Which of the religions do you imagine our Father supports over the others? Which medical journal does our Father suggest will best help us to heal His children? Regarding politics, do you believe our all-knowing Father will likely be a Republican or a Democrat?

Q: I see what you mean. We insist on using human-made theology to guess at the will of God, science to explain the universe, and politics to organize ourselves with efficiency and fairness for all. We do this knowing none of these approaches have accomplished those goals nearly as well as Jesus showed us was possible.

A: I am not suggesting that humankind immediately do away with religion, science, and politics. Eventually, that will work, but many adjustments to our shared worldview are needed before such major changes succeed. We indeed have flawed religions and governments with limited science, but they reflect our shared consciousness today. When we lovingly use what we already have, the improvements will come, and more will be given to us.

Q: Your explanation reminds me of my military training admonishing, "Do something, even if it's wrong!"

A: And to that, I would answer, "Out of the mouths of babes." To be good for something, you must be doing something." "It is far easier to correct the course of anything in motion than to start it moving from a dead stop." There is great truth in such clichés.

Q: I'm not sure what you meant before when you said, "*We indeed have flawed religions and government with quite limited science, but they all reflect our shared consciousness as it stands today.*"

A: The state of the world today is the result of our combined thoughts and choices. We deserve the leaders we have and the limitations of our technology to help resolve our challenges.

Q: Does that mean the German people of WWII deserved Hitler?

A: To answer "yes" to that question would be misleading from humanity's perspective, but "yes" is still the short answer. To help understand this better, let me say that the whole world helped bring Hitler to power. Up until his motives turned Imperialistic and genocidal, Hitler accomplished a great deal of good for the German people. Once Hitler stepped onto the slippery slope of selfishness and lost track of his original purpose, his choices took him ever further away from the loving ways of our Father.

Q: What about Hitler's attempted genocide of the Jews?

A: Hitler ended up there after starting down what seemed a far less murderous path. Initially, he preferred that the Jews leave Germany. Other countries did not allow the Jews to immigrate except for the wealthy elite among them. The Jews were not popular with most Christians and Muslims going back centuries before WWII. Any measurement of selfishness using the number of senseless deaths attributed to the policies of a country's leader puts the spotlight on Stalin more than Hitler. Stalin, too, came to power and decided that "his ends justified his means."

Q: Historically speaking, Stalin seems to take a back seat to Hitler when naming infamous despots because Hitler opposed all of Russia, much of Europe as well as the US. Is that an example of the old cliché, "The enemy of my enemy is my friend"?

A: Essentially, that is correct. Many political agreements are arranged because selfish motives result in unholy alliances. This is why government and politics, as they are today, are unlikely ever to reach a loving solution. Compromising the selfish desires of each participant rarely ends up with a win/win solution. Often, it turns out to be the opposite.

Q: But you speak of cooperation as a key component of our spiritual growth. Can you clarify what you are suggesting we do?

A: Cooperation is where everyone involved experiences a win/win outcome because all negotiations are done with the intention of love, patience, and goodwill. Compromise is where no one gets what they truly want because their talks are based on selfish intentions, which logically lead to flawed solutions. These definitions are not those found in the dictionary.

Q: Can you offer a specific example of how that works in real life?

A: Of course. A good example occurred when this country's government voted to approve Prohibition. Two of the greatest supporters of making alcohol illegal were the religious groups against drinking and the bootleggers who would profit greatly by making it illegal. The politicians, bowing to the pressure of that uneasy alliance, passed a law taking away the option of drinking alcohol even though so many citizens had already decided it was okay to drink.

Q: But I don't see that "alliance" as more than a coincidence of their agendas rather than resulting from a selfish negotiation. Surely you understand my confusion?

A: It will become clear in a moment, but first, let me finish setting the stage. In politics, it is said that to know what's really going on, you should follow the power and money. When it comes to understanding the will of our Father, we should always follow the loving path. If the religions were trying to coerce Prohibition into law, would that seem to be motivated by power, money, or love?

Q: I would say that was motivated more by power, as in forcing others to live as they preferred the world to be.

A: And the motivation for the bootleggers' support of Prohibition?

Q: That was clearly because of the money they would make through illegal alcohol sales.

A: Was Prohibition considered a success in changing how society felt about alcohol?

Q: No, it wasn't. It was repealed less than 15 years after becoming the law. Why is that?

A: We cannot legislate morality, especially with selfish motives, and expect lasting success. To lovingly win over the hearts and minds of the people to agree upon a lasting solution is the better way for all concerned. The people of this country had already decided to drink alcohol. Prohibition became law because politicians wanted the support of the religions (power) and bootleggers (money) to get re-elected. Those combined selfish motives largely explain why Prohibition came to be law and yet did not succeed.

Q: So you're saying between the church's desire to force people to stop drinking and the bootleggers' desire to profit from people drinking regardless, along with the politicians' desire to get re-elected, Prohibition was doomed from the start?

A: Yes. Prohibition was seen as the solution, but it was the lowest common denominator compromise of the selfish desires and motivations of those who helped make it become law.

Q: But we still haven't achieved a good societal balance regarding everyone's drinking habits. It seems that eliminating Prohibition didn't work either. What is the answer?

A: A good example of what does work is the current campaign against smoking. The percentage of smokers in this country just 50 years ago was much higher than it is today. While laws restricting where smoking can occur have been implemented, no one outlawed smoking as they did with alcohol. This "culture change" against smoking has been slow but sure and will eventually succeed.

Q: So we should have done the same thing to discourage drinking alcohol as we have been doing to discourage smoking?

A: That has already started with the advertising campaigns against driving drunk. The people who want to change other people's drinking habits are learning that coercion doesn't work better than telling the truth to gain people's support and compliance.

Q: I understand and agree with your point. However, what about our efforts to help the poor, educate the masses, and provide for the common good? Is that the role of government, and don't they often have to "legislate morality" to accomplish that goal?

A: Not by using the perspective you just offered. Being our neighbor's keeper is better achieved when it becomes the voluntary desire of each person. The moment we believe government programs are the best way to care for others instead of each of us taking personal responsibility to help, we have lost sight of the goal. Study the efficiency and caring of many non-profit organizations in helping their neighbors compared to that of most government programs to see the truth of this.

Q: So it is not enough to write a check to help others? Are you saying we all should also personally serve in soup kitchens?

A: There are many ways to give and be of service, but it should be done with joy and balance. We are urged to give our money, time, and talents to care for our neighbors. To offer others less than a tithe of all our gifts would be out of balance with the way that our Father gives to us. And no, choosing to write a bigger check to avoid volunteering or volunteering more hours to avoid giving up our money does not make for the balance I mentioned.

Q: You said politics is about money and power, so let's discuss taxes. What is the fairest way for us to create a revenue system to fund our government and all it does?

A: That starts with the assumption that the government's role should be so large. The government will become a minor societal voice when love is our guide. Taxes will be quite low compared to today because our citizens will locally volunteer and donate money to meet everyone's needs. The government legislating mandatory taxes will no longer be necessary.

Q: It seems Jesus rising from the dead was probably no greater miracle than getting people to willingly donate the same money they now pay in mandatory taxes. How could that ever happen? Are we heading toward a communistic style of government in the future?

A: Let me be clear regarding any existing form of government or political system is the answer we seek for world peace. If everyone makes loving choices at every opportunity, then any system of government can succeed. If there were seven billion people with the Christ consciousness populating the earth, how could they help but be happy and prosperous regardless of the government in charge? However, if we continue to make selfish choices, then no system of government will result in happiness for all.

Q: My head spins, thinking of how a completely loving population will ever come to be. Are you sure that's where we're headed?

A: Our Father has already given the Promised Land to His people. How does everyone become part of His chosen people? In the truest sense, we already are. But we will need patience, cooperation, and a shared worldview to recognize and receive His wondrous gift. The only thing that stands in our way is our free will. Rest assured that we will not choose to resist our Father's loving ways forever.

Q: Can you clarify what you meant about the role of government and taxes in the future?

A: Think for a moment of a world where everyone is their neighbor's keeper. Who would be homeless in a world like that? Who would go hungry? Would anyone be turned away from medical care for lacking money? When people make only loving decisions, no one ever suffers from their needs being ignored. If all of the world's disadvantaged people are taken care of at the local level through various non-profit organizations, what need is there for compulsory national government programs to help them?

Q: I see where this is going, given that well over half our federal budget funds the military and other means of defense. If there were no wars or other kinds of violent conflicts, do we need to spend so much money protecting us from ourselves?

A: That's the shared vision that lies in our future! It is because our fear persists, and we have a lack of trust in others that motivates us to spend so much money defensively. Would war ever be necessary if all nations were convinced that everyone would cooperate with love and efficiency in resolving any conflict or inequity?

Q: Well, what if the conflict was due to religious differences? We've had more than a few wars based on those.

A: There are kind, gentle, peace-loving followers of every major religion. If that understanding spreads to all people, what religions would not get along, let alone believe that a war could resolve their differences?

Q: That all seems so far off, if not nearly impossible, to accomplish.

A: Making this kind of progress is often deceiving when only looking at our daily news sources. While it may be difficult to see now, humankind is changing its worldview for the better. We are quickly improving as we each become the change we desire to see in the world.

Q: But how do we get from where we are now to the wonderful vision you just offered for the future?

A: As we each choose His loving ways for our own, the world is changing one soul at a time for the better. This is happening quietly everywhere despite what is shown on the news and on websites. People will soon find that many others share their hope for peace and goodwill more than a desire to take advantage. Once we start to love and trust each other, the vicious cycle downward reverses at an amazing rate.

Q: You've made so many questions I thought I'd be asking moot with this "loving new world view" approach. Questions like, "Who should we elect to government?" How should we fairly tax everyone? What about immigration policies? Is a continued military presence in other countries a good idea? What role should the government play in overseeing medical care and retirement funds? I have many more such questions, but your answers take us away from politics as a solution.

A: The political controversies we face today are symptoms of the fundamental challenges before us. Thinking we can elect the right people or pass better laws to make everything right does not address the real challenge. We have forgotten that with our Father, all things are possible.

Q: But if we had the right people in government and they passed the perfect set of laws, wouldn't that set us on the right course?

A: I am so glad you asked that question. It brings up the perfect situation in history to make the point. This story happened long ago in Egypt. The ruler who came to power at that time was called Aknaughton. He was the first political leader of that time who believed in our loving Father as the First Cause behind all creation. He decreed laws supporting this loving perspective and commanded everyone to worship our Father as the only deity. The people and land prospered during Aknaughton's reign as never before. Ultimately, those who opposed Aknaughton's new order assassinated him. It did not take long for the people and land to revert to their chaotic position before Aknaughton came to power.

Q: The point is that success will be temporary if we try to legislate morality, even with the best intentions.

A: Just so. This is an important lesson, and knowing that it was carried out with almost total control over the people, as Aknaughton had, helped prove the point. Without understanding this lesson, most people continue to believe our highest priority should be to get the right people elected so that they can create the perfect laws to set all things in order. What is largely unknown is that coercing others, even when forced to do things "perfectly," might last for a while, but those changes will not endure.

Q: I see why we must first make the desired changes from within. It is the changes we decide upon for ourselves that stick. In closing, are there words of loving encouragement you would share on these issues?

A: Anyone who doubts that a perfect win/win outcome is forthcoming has lost faith in our perfect Father and neighbors. In truth, we are not learning anything new. We remember who we are and what we are already capable of doing. On earth, it is said that only death and taxes are inevitable. In truth, nothing but our Father's love prevails for eternity.

Helen Ruth's Most Embarrassing Moment

It was 1959, and my mother, Helen Ruth, was attending her first conference in Virginia Beach. This conference was held at the headquarters of the Edgar Cayce organization, the Association for Research and Enlightenment (A.R.E.). Helen Ruth was an enthusiastic student and was asked to lead a group meditation the following day. She accepted, but she did not feel prepared.

She located the Edgar Cayce Readings on Meditation and studied them that night. Her preparation kept her up until the wee hours of the morning, and she only slept for a few hours before the alarm went off. The subject of the first class was Dreams, and it was going to be presented by Herb, the director of education for the A.R.E. Helen Ruth didn't want to miss Herb's class despite her lack of sleep the night before.

It turned out that Herb sat down next to my mother that same morning to eat breakfast in the cafeteria. She had two cups of coffee on her tray, and Herb asked her why. Helen Ruth responded, "I've so been looking forward to your class this morning, and I wanted to make sure I didn't fall asleep!" Herb graciously allowed the gaff to pass by without comment.

Despite her embarrassing start with Herb, Helen Ruth soon made dream interpretation, prayer, and meditation a daily part of her life. In case you're wondering, she remained friends with Herb for decades afterward.

Meditation and Prayer

Q: There are many viewpoints regarding meditation and prayer. Some even feel meditation can be dangerous. What value is there in these long-held spiritual practices?

A: Some people teach that both prayer and meditation are the practice of quieting the mind to connect with an outside spiritual consciousness. Some think that it is getting in touch with our own higher self. Others believe it is a way to communicate with souls who are no longer in human bodies. More still believe this is how we communicate directly with our Father. Some think meditation is used to communicate with evil of many types.

Q: And which of those is most correct?

A: Prayer in conjunction with meditation is the best way to connect with the Holy Spirit within. Communicating with evil is never a part of prayer or meditation.

Q: Some people are convinced that mediation is a way to communicate with evil beings. Why do you say that is not the case?

A: When done correctly, meditation is humans' safest communication with the divine within. No evil is allowed to interfere when the soul has lovingly asked to receive only the highest guidance while being protected from any hindrance.

Q: Are there special words we should use to invoke God's protection when we meditate?

A: Prayers of protection should always precede meditation. The Lord's Prayer is good, but any appropriate words thought or said with the highest intention will work well. Also, visualize all but the highest good vanishing from the sacred space around you as you enter into the Holy of Holies. There is no greater spiritual protection than this for all.

Q: So prayers of protection and attunement should always come before meditating. And what are the advantages of meditating?

A: Through meditation, we achieve greater balance in the body, mind, and soul. If you think of an electrical circuit, the power raised through meditation is like electricity flowing without interruption. The better we connect with the divine, the better choices we make. The better choices we make, the better mental and physical health we enjoy.

Q: There seem to be many methods of meditation. Most involve focusing on something like words, movement, or an object. Are all these techniques doing the same thing for us?

A: In an overall sense, yes. However, similar to how medical doctors specialize in healing the body, different meditation methods excel in bringing us into balance where we specifically need help. Each meditation method you mentioned serves a specific purpose in bringing about balance.

Q: I'll guess that meditations that focus on movement, such as yoga or Tai Chi, help to bring the physical into balance. Using our eyes to focus on an object like a candle flame helps balance us mentally. And using words or a mantra helps put our physical and mental aspects into better balance with our higher spiritual self.

A: Well said! You covered all meditative techniques with a rather broad brush stroke, but those approaches generally help as you indicated.

Q: What is the ideal form of meditation?

A: The one we will use daily.

Q: I was thinking more about what method would be the most effective for us.

A: The best answer to your question is still the one we will use daily. You thought there might be a hierarchy of all the meditation techniques, where we should start with one and move up through an established order as we progress.

Q: That would seem logical. Isn't that how it works?

A: In one sense, yes, but no two people will respond to the various meditation techniques in the same way. We are each individual, and our spiritual paths are not linear. As it is with most things, we will be given the next steps on our path when we apply what we already know.

Q: So there are no general "best practices" regarding meditation?

A: There are, but they won't be the same for everyone. Generally speaking, study the three approaches (physical, mental, or spiritual) and see which one appeals to you the most, then begin each day with it.

Q: I have noticed that various breathing techniques are a part of almost every form of meditation. Why is that?

A: The goal of meditation is to achieve a balance in the energy flow between the physical, mental, and spiritual aspects of self. Breathing is controlled either consciously or by the autonomic part of the mind. Breathing is a natural connection point between the conscious and subconscious (physical and mental) aspects of the soul. Purposefully regulating our breathing allows us to synchronize our subconscious minds with the conscious.

Q: What would be the best path for me to follow for progressive meditation techniques?

A: You, like many, came into this life having practiced meditation already. Given your historic preference, the physical movement meditations would not work so well for you. Neither would visually concentrate on an object and using that technique would not allow your active mind to remain focused for long. Even focusing on a spiritual mantra does not work as well to keep your mind and intention, which is where meditation can aid you the most.

Q: That is true. I remember starting with my eyes closed using a lovingly worded mantra meditation and found it didn't work very well for me.

A: You tried to jump too far ahead from the start. Simply focusing on an affirmation of love did not fill and satisfy your mind with what it needed to remain focused. Only when you learned another technique did you begin to enjoy meditation.

Q: Go ahead and talk through what finally worked for me.

A: If the whole point of meditation is to raise our consciousness so that the body/mind/spirit is attuned and in balance, you found that focusing on thoughts of your happiest memories brought that about. Your "mantra" was remembering what it is like to be loved, happy, and of great service to others. Some people use words, but it works better for you to use your best memories.

Q: I must say that I've never been able to move on from that method. I still use it today. Does that show a lack of progress?

A: A lack of progress is when we stop meditating. We've already covered that the best meditation method is the one that we will use consistently. You have found the way that works for you. It is because you are able to attune to and focus on the divine within through loving, joyous thoughts that we can communicate as we are doing now.

Q: In a general sense, I understand that we raise our consciousness to a higher level during meditation. What is happening within the body during meditation?

A: Eastern philosophies refer to the spiritual energy raised as the kundalini. It follows the path of the seven spiritual centers or chakras in the body as it rises. As the energy passes through each center, it purifies and refreshes while the chakras steadily increase in vibration. At its peak, we can have what is often called a "white light experience." As the energy passes through the pineal gland and moves to the pituitary, our cup literally "runneth over," as given in the 23rd Psalm. The glandular secretions during meditation at that level can be experienced as seeing a beautiful white light or bringing about spiritual visions to aid, encourage, and comfort us.

Q: What is that word, kundalini?

A: It is a Sanskrit word meaning coiled energy. It is a powerful healing archetype, as depicted in the medical symbol called the caduceus with the coiled serpents encircling a staff. The spiritual energy moves up through the chakras in a similar manner. It is up to us to channel this energy by serving others physically, mentally, and spiritually.

Q: If I understand the process correctly, we begin with a prayer of protection and spiritual cleansing. Then, we enter into meditation using whatever method works best for us. How should we close our meditation session?

A: Close as you started, with prayer. Start by offering the energies raised in meditation as healing or support toward those we know and love or for others who have requested it, such as names on a prayer list. Raising such powerful spiritual energies within us and not releasing them through healing or supportive prayers for others can agitate our bodies and unsettle our minds.

Think of how we had felt after a tremendous scare when a lot of adrenaline was released in the body, and then we realized there was no danger. While the body can work to counteract the adrenaline, it is unsettling while it flows through our system, and we do nothing to use it.

Q: You said we should release the energies through healing or support? Why the distinction? Shouldn't we always pray that someone be healed?

A: That is not our choice to make. Praying to heal someone when they have set a different path for themselves can interfere with their free will. When a body is out of balance by the individual's choice, either karmically or to set up conditions for lessons to be learned, praying to heal the condition before they are ready to be healed can work in opposition to their highest good.

Q: Like a stubborn child who will deny what they need most to spite those who upset them?

A: That analogy works well enough. Both children and adults do not enjoy being forced, even into things for their benefit, like good health.

Q: But Jesus healed people all the time. Wasn't He interfering with their free will in the way you just mentioned?

A: Not at all. Jesus only offered His healing prayers to those who willingly consented. It should not surprise you that Jesus was communicating with those He helped to heal at all levels, physical/mental/spiritual. That multi-level "consent" always took place, though most of the people witnessing those healings only recognized what occurred in the physical.

Q: I remember it was said that Jesus could perform no miracles in Nazareth because they didn't believe the same boy they saw growing up was the Holy Spirit incarnate. Is "having faith they will be healed" what you mean by needing their consent?

A: Yes, but there is more to it than that. What is not mentioned in the Bible is that many of the people who Jesus helped heal did not remain so in that or in future lifetimes. We can start with the best of intentions and not follow through all the way.

Q: Why is that?

A: Healing works similarly to the story of Peter walking on the water with Jesus. Each person's ability to maintain the level of love, faith, and trust that allows such "miracles" to manifest can fade over time. While love conquers all, if we have not made the permanent changes in our thinking that brought the health imbalance, to begin with, then even the healings Jesus facilitated will be temporary.

Q: That explains why God does not interfere with our free will. All it does is delay the inevitable day when we must freely choose His loving ways for our own. Healing our infirmities, poverty, or relationships will not last if we don't understand how we got out of balance in the first place.

A: Nicely put. If we have willingly made choices that put us out of accord with our Father's loving ways, we must learn where we went astray before we know what to adjust in our thinking. Any changes we make or ailments healed that don't lovingly align our physical/mental/soul levels are essentially cosmetic and will not last.

Q: I noticed that you mentioned Jesus offered healing prayers rather than actually healing people. Can you explain that further?

A: That wording is correct. Jesus healed no one. But He did provide the spiritual energy by which the individuals could heal themselves if they willingly accepted the power and help He offered.

Q: Describing the healing process Jesus used as prayer is a new concept for me. I always looked at what we do for others as a healing prayer, whereas Jesus healed people.

A: Your confusion is one of the reasons why we have trouble believing we can all do what Jesus did and greater. The prayers of Jesus are no more powerful than our own except for how perfectly His will aligns with our Father's on the physical/mental/spiritual levels. Our ability to align our will with His is the measure of our access to His knowledge and power, as well as being able to channel the same to others to aid in healing.

Q: You mentioned God, Jesus, and the Holy Spirit and often said "His" without distinguishing which of those three you meant. Does that matter?

A: No. They are all the same in essence and purpose.

Q: You have defined meditation in detail already. Can you offer more information regarding how prayer works?

A: Simply said, prayer is speaking to our Father, while meditation is listening to Him.

Q: By speaking to God, do you mean that our prayers somehow cajole or convince God to do what we ask?

A: You already know that's false, but many see prayer differently. In truth, prayer and meditation are two sides of the same communication coin. We should not just speak to our Father. We should listen to Him as well.

Q: Is there such a thing as too much listening and not enough speaking to God?

A: This is possible. We are not meant to be passive in the choices we make. Our Father desires that His children freely and lovingly choose what they want. Ideally, we make those choices in perfect accord with His loving ways. Removing ourselves so completely from making decisions that we virtually cease to exist is possible. Declining to make choices in hopes of passing all responsibility over to God can be a sin of omission.

Q: I remember basic training in the military when the trainees were told to "do something, even if it's wrong." Is that the idea?

A: Correct. Though we might make a wrong choice, the momentum of our good intentions will guide us toward a right and loving path. Little progress is made when we completely give up our role in choosing what should come next for us.

Q: But if "we only do what we see our Father doing," doesn't that mean we should only choose what God suggests?

A: Since there is rarely just one way to resolve any conflict lovingly, the guidance we receive from our Father will offer many options, all of which would be in harmony with His will. Our job is to discern which options will bring the best outcome and the greatest joy to all concerned, including us. Our having free will places the responsibility on us to decide which choice we prefer of all those available. As long as we are open to accepting a better solution from our Father, all bases are covered.

Q: So, how does prayer work if we are not changing God's mind or causing Him to take action on our requests?

A: In a real sense, prayer makes our decisions an active and cooperative effort with the Holy Spirit rather than simply reacting to whatever happens to us. Through prayer, we begin to raise the energies within and align with the highest level of consciousness we can. If doing what Jesus would do is not something we can accomplish, then we will receive guidance appropriate for what we are able to do. That guidance takes into account where we are mentally so that our suggested actions always align with our Father's will.

Q: Prayer doesn't change anything but ourselves.

A: That is correct but with one rather astonishing exception. Prayers often help to change the conditions around us.

Q: Can you give me an example?

A: Say a church board is looking to buy a new location. Their research comes down to two properties, each with strengths and weaknesses. The board starts out split on which of them is the better choice. However, they persevere, and through a patient, cooperative effort, they agree upon one of the two properties. Even if the property they end up choosing began as the lesser of those two, the board's loving efforts in reaching that decision would literally change the worldly conditions. In that way, the "lesser property" chosen through patience and love would ultimately be the better investment.

Q: That's quite a concept! Are you saying we can't make a wrong decision when working for a good cause?

A: No. Had the church board allowed their personal biases and selfishness to influence the decision-making process, the opposite result would occur. In that way, the board could have chosen the better property and had it turn out to be the lesser of the two. All our thoughts work like prayers, but only our loving thoughts work for the lasting good of all concerned.

Q: Do our prayers help God to know what we want?

A: No, but they help us clarify what we want. Our prayers are not for the benefit of our Father, for you are correct that He knows our thoughts at every moment. In truth, our Father does not directly answer our prayers. He instead designed the universal laws to ensure that all of existence rearranges itself to automatically adjust to the free will choices every one of us makes.

Q: Now, that was a mouthful. Are you saying the universe changes every time we make a choice?

A: Yes. This is not as difficult to understand as you might think. If you imagine a lake of very still water and drop a pebble into its center, you can visualize the ripples that would affect the entire surface. If you do the same with one or even seven billion pebbles, will not every one of those ripples still affect the whole? The water will seek balance for every new wave. In the same way, the choices we make always seek balance throughout the fabric of space, time, and all of creation.

Q: That's pretty heavy stuff. Can you explain more about why God doesn't directly answer our prayers?

A: Of course. Our Father never stops loving, encouraging, guiding, and supporting us in every way we allow. What prayer does is put ourselves in better accord with His loving ways, which help us accept all He continuously offers us. In that way, our Father is not directly answering our prayers; instead, we are opening our hearts and minds through prayer to receive our fill of His abundance.

Q: This is a new way of understanding how prayer works. You already said that prayers of protection should be done at the start of each meditation. I used to envision that as a white light descending to envelop and protect me as I entered the Holy of Holies. Would it be better to visualize myself being raised and surrounded by God's love for protection and the highest guidance?

A: That image will work for many, but this is especially true for you. It better reflects the true nature of prayer and even the reality of raising the individual's consciousness rather than lowering our Father's love to His children. Such is the way prayer works in our lives.

Q: I understand prayer raises our consciousness, but what do our prayers do for others?

A: Envision your prayers, holding the person as if they were enveloped in love. Much of the struggle for anyone working through a difficult situation occurs when they do not feel loved and supported. Surrounding them with your prayers is a great way to help people to heal themselves. This works because you are providing a safe and loving "cocoon" to support them while they correct their imbalance.

Q: When is it appropriate to offer healing prayers, and when should they be supportive?

A: Healing prayers are appropriate if the person you are praying for has requested healing. If that is not clear, then supportive prayers are appropriate.

Q: Aren't some people more adept at facilitating healing through prayer than others?

A: Of course, but it is easy to forget the source of all healing. Thinking that people who offer a "laying on of hands" are the ones who healed another person is never correct, yet it is also a common perspective. This is often misunderstood by the people healed, those who watched them be healed, and even the "healers" themselves. This is not all that different compared to some medical doctors who believe they are the reason a patient is healed.

Q: What happens when people pray for less-than-loving outcomes? Say the prayers are for an ex-spouse to be unhappy in their next relationship or pray that someone competing for the same promotion becomes ill. Do those prayers work despite the selfish intent behind them?

A: "Do all our thoughts and prayers have the intended effect?" is a better way of asking that question. The answer is "yes" in that all our thoughts act as messengers of the energy sent out and will have an effect according to our intention.

Think of our thoughts combined as votes for a particular piece of legislation or political candidate when trying to understand this cumulative effect on a country or even the planet.

However, it would not be correct to group our unloving thoughts with our loving ones and call them all prayers. Again, it is important to say that we are always protected from negative energies when we ask to be. That is another reason why daily prayer and meditation is so important for us to remain balanced.

Q: Negative prayers sound like witchcraft or black magic. Are they related?

A: Loving thoughts that serve to do the will of our Father are what prayer was intended to be. Our selfish thoughts still send out vibrations (like ripples or waves in the water) that can temporarily affect conditions in the way we desire. Loving thoughts and prayers are always stronger. An organized effort of thoughts/prayers to serve a selfish end is sad indeed, but souls often become confused as to which is greater: a loving intention or selfish actions.

Q: Let's end this on a bright note. What closing words do you have for us on prayer and meditation?

A: If we truly understood how powerful prayer is in helping ourselves and others, we would feel motivated to pray without ceasing. Being a channel for our Father's supportive and healing energies cleanses and revitalizes us as we share it with others. Through prayer, we begin to understand the true abundance that lies in the power of love. As it is with a rising tide, "prayer floats everyone's boat," so to speak. We should be sure that our prayers always ask for "this or better" so we do not tie our own hands in how we can accept His help.

Meditation is when we approach our most natural state of consciousness. This is when we allow the conscious mind to be quieted and instead listen to the still, small voice within. Meditation is the best and easiest way to fulfill Christ's promises in our lives. How can we do that? Always meditate with the expectation that we will receive the answers we seek as we remember the words of Jesus: Ask, and it shall be given, seek and we shall find, knock and it shall be opened unto us. When we ask for anything from a loving intention (in His name), it shall be ours.

A Colorful Army

I sat in well-worn wooden bleachers with 200 fellow soldiers in the mid-1970s. We were receiving a briefing on our first day of basic training in the Army. The drill sergeant, as our gracious host over the next couple of months, covered the "dos and don'ts" of our stay with him. He held our attention more because of his down-to-earth sense of humor than the content of his words.

Suddenly, his tone turned serious as he began to speak about prejudice and how it has no place in the US Army. He said he knew everything about life "back on the block." He knew that people of different races didn't make friends easily and didn't mix at all in many parts of the US. He emphasized that none of that "prejudice stuff" would fly in the Army and especially in "Charlie" company. He said there was only one skin color in the Army: green. No white, black, brown, yellow, or red...only green, like everything else in the Army.

While I had been raised to think positively of racial differences, I had not before been in a group where I was in the minority of skin color. In our short time together in the Army, I had already experienced prejudice directed at me because I was different. I wondered how the others in the bleachers were taking the drill sergeant's admonishments against such thinking.

I had my answer a moment later. The drill sergeant concluded his introductory comments and yelled for us to line up in formation. He added, "All the light green guys need to line up on my left with the dark green guys to my right." The resulting laughter showed they shared his conflicted perspective. He was kidding, of course, but most of what I learned about the ugly side of prejudice between races came from my time in the Army.

And with that anecdote, the chapter on bigotry follows.

Bigotry

Q: I have always wondered why people are biased against others because of their race, religion, or what have you.

A: Bigotry against others arises in many forms, but it always comes down to low self-esteem and fear. When we recognize and honor the Oneness of all things, we put aside the feelings that would separate anyone or anything from the Whole.

Q: But why does prejudice occur in so many different ways? Some people hate others for their spiritual beliefs, others for their skin color, and others still for their political preferences.

A: This concerns the old cliché of the chain's weakest link. Our selfishness will manifest wherever we are the weakest in our thoughts regarding love, faith, patience, trust, and forgiveness.

Q: So, how did bigotry get started in the first place?

A: As I said, fear and low self-esteem were the first motivations. If we are unhappy with ourselves, we blame and fear others as the cause. Once we fear other people, making them the target of our selfish biases becomes easier.

Q: But what about slavery? Surely we don't fear people we enslave?

A: From a fearful and limited perspective, what better way to feel good about ourselves than to put others down? That is the self-esteem part of our motivation toward bigotry. The fear comes from our inner knowing that we are all One and that we will reap the bigotry we sow through our selfishness. Oftentimes, that occurs at the hands of those we caused to suffer in the first place. So yes, being afraid of those we enslave is not only common, it is even warranted from a karmic perspective.

Q: So if we are prejudiced against people because of their religion in one life, does that always come back to us karmically in another life as religious bigotry?

A: Often, that is true. Overcoming bigotry karmicly occurs in the same way it began. The optimistic way of seeing this helps with the lesson. If we discriminate against others because of their religion, race, gender, political or sexual preferences, we are given an opportunity to learn that we are all One. Mistreating others for any reason makes no sense from our Father's loving perspective.

Q: And yet bigotry continues in each of those areas. Are we learning anything?

A: Without question, the world is getting better in this regard. If we would prefer to only look at examples that indicate bigotry is alive and well, that is our choice to make. However, we only have to look at how we treat each other in times of war and afterward today, compared to thousands of years ago, to see we are improving.

Q: But doesn't having free will also mean we should not "legislate morality?" You said we cannot force people into thinking and acting lovingly by passing laws and making rules.

A: This is correct. If making rules and passing laws against bigotry were the only efforts made, very little would have changed all this time. However, every soul intuitively knows we are all One. Even when we choose to ignore that truth, we are continually guided by our Father's love to accept everyone as a divine sibling. It might be said that humankind is getting better despite the desires of some to coerce the thoughts and actions of others.

Q: So, should we or should we not have laws on the books regarding bigotry?

A: Making or doing away with such laws is not the point. It will still come down to the resentment of some to be forced to act a certain way compared to freely choosing to treat others according to the law of love. As Paul said in the Bible, we can sacrifice our lives for others, but if we do so without love as motivation, it counts for nothing.

Q: I understand that part, but if the laws humans create only support our choices through unconditional love, what is wrong with keeping those?

A: The laws humans make are not the real challenge. It is the intention we hold behind creating those laws that indicate a loving intent or a desire to force others to act as we would prefer. Without a loving intention behind our laws, even with careful wording, they will not accomplish the goal. The words of Paul in the Bible have been used to condone both slavery and bigotry. Paul also offered a most beautiful and detailed description of love. We each must choose for ourselves which path leads us back to the Father

Q: But so many people live their lives according to what is established as "legal." Shouldn't society set a standard for our behavior consistent with Jesus's life as our role model?

A: There is a big difference between the awareness and choices available to someone perfect in the Christ Consciousness compared to those of us who currently have a more limited perspective. Often, it is enough progress for us to take the first step forward rather than expect perfection.

Q: Can you give me an example of what you mean?

A: In speaking of bigotry, let me use an example of the plight of humans with dark skin in the Deep South after the Civil War. From today's greater understanding of bigotry, we look back at those times and shake our heads. However, in years to come, when prejudice is no longer a factor, society will look back on these current times and see that prejudice still exists. The ultimate goal is unconditional love and equality for everyone, but we get there one step at a time.

First, stop enslaving people, then stop the violence against them; then stop believing "separate but equal" is the best answer; then stop quietly discriminating, and eventually, we end up achieving the intended goal. Using that rough timeline, you can see room for improvement.

Q: Why is it that we tend to learn everything so slowly? It would seem that once we understand that every human is an unconditionally loved child of God, bigotry will disappear from that point forward.

A: Some catch the entire concept at once: "Go forth and sin no more." Others work through their deep prejudices as though they were peeling back the layers of an onion. It can bring tears and suffering, but persevering will not make them disappointed in the person they become. We all make progress in accord with what is right for us.

Q: Is that to say that no progress was made regarding bigotry and slavery until after the Civil War?

A: Progress is always made if we continually look for the good in everything. Even our selfish acts are included among the steps we take to return to our Father if we choose to see it that way.

Q: But what is the quickest way to show someone the futility of being a bigot?

A: It is easier if they believe in reincarnation, karma, and grace. By simply knowing that we have already been and will likely be again all the genders, races, and religions we might choose to discriminate against, whom should we hate that does not include ourselves? Knowing that we will reap any bigotry we sow means that in future lives, we might well become the very people we would discriminate against today. That is quite compelling for most people, assuming they believe in reincarnation.

Q: And if they don't believe in reincarnation?

A: Then treating even "the least of these" as if they were Christ is another good approach. Regardless of their spiritual outlook and beliefs, all the major religions have similar teachings regarding the loving way we should treat one another.

Q: To say that some people qualify to be called the "least of these" doesn't feel right. How do you reconcile there being a hierarchy of souls when God loves us all equally?

A: Jesus Himself was seen as "the least of these" by those who opposed His teachings. The truth is that even the Christ Consciousness incarnate can still qualify as being "the least of these" to someone. So the focus of that statement was not implying that our Father created a hierarchy of souls but rather that treating everyone with love and respect leads to a better understanding of the Oneness of all.

Q: I see your point. No matter how spiritually advanced we are or how loving we might be, we can still be perceived as a heretic according to the standards of other people. However, I'm still confused about how people could be "good Christians" and still have bigotry in their hearts.

A: Humans often allow religion to become a stumbling block rather than serving as a stepping stone. Consider the ongoing conflict between the Muslims and the Jews. Compare that to WWII's past conflict between Japan and the United States. What can we learn from contrasting those two examples?

Q: The Muslims and Jews have been at each other's throats for many centuries, and all in the name of Allah or God. There seems to be no end to their fighting. Even though great atrocities took place during WWII between Japan and the US, they are now strong allies both economically and politically. The healing between those two nations took place in less than 50 years compared to the Muslims and Jews who have yet to work out their differences. I cannot figure out why one conflict has healed and the other, so far, has not. What is the answer?

A: Both the Muslims and Jews believe they are the chosen people of our Father. That implies that any people not of our religion, in effect, are not as worthy of our Father's love. Once we believe we can determine a person or group's "worthiness" in our Father's eyes, the seeds of bigotry have taken root. If we are not personally involved, it doesn't take much to see that there is little hope in resolving differences using religion and politics as tools for healing.

Q: But Buddhists and Christians are very different from each other. Why were they able to work out their differences where the Muslims and Jews have not?

A: The separation of church and state is a helpful step in allowing each person to forgive and heal. As often happens when a nation combines spirituality with politics, all transgressions against them by the perceived "enemy" are affronts against the one true God they believe in. We can more easily forgive transgressions against ourselves than we can those sins we perceive as committed against our God.

Q: Interesting! So, Japan and the US were able to heal faster because God was not perceived as being involved in each side's transgressions against the other. So, is it always asking for trouble to mix religion and politics?

A: It can be, but that depends on the individual. If every citizen was filled with the Christ Spirit and only made choices from love, what religion or political system could fail in such a case? If the citizens always made selfish choices based on fear, what religion or political system could succeed in supporting such people? Keeping church and state separate would be better if a nation's people find themselves somewhere short of perfection.

Q: It occurs to me that there is silent bigotry in any religion that teaches of an irreversible hell. Those souls who might be judged unworthy of entering into heaven inevitably are viewed as outcasts or "the least of these" by others who consider themselves "saved."

A: Hell is never irreversible, but our suffering can be eternal if that is what we choose. Our Father never desires for us to suffer nor even to be sad or discouraged. Still, your point is good that believing in an irreversible hell goes against the teachings of endless forgiveness and our Father's unconditional love for all souls. A perceived hierarchy of souls is inevitable if we believe our Father would condemn any of us.

Q: So how do people who believe in a loving God reconcile supporting a church where only their own race of humans feel welcome to attend?

A: If you were to ask those who prefer being with humans of their own race, you would find that they do not ponder such questions. In their minds, everyone can go to heaven, but the implication is that each will continue to "keep to their own kind." For some who believe in reincarnation, you would find that choosing a church with a representative mix of races in the membership isn't a high priority for them. We often don't consider such questions if we are not personally affected by the issue. Ignoring bigotry that does not affect us can be selfish in itself, but it is common nonetheless.

Q: To end bigotry, we should start by consciously identifying all the places where it exists.

A: That approach could work but is too analytical for most. Almost everyone entrapped on the earth is prejudiced in some way. When we hold ill feelings toward others because they broke "our rules," we are out of harmony with our Father's loving ways. People condemn others for such things as infidelity in marriage, cheating on their taxes, lying, and not following through on their promises.

Q: But those are examples of people making a deliberate poor choice. Discrimination against people because of their age, race, sexual preference, religion, gender, and those sorts of things are the areas we should not stand in judgment of … right?

A: To judge others is a very different thing than to condemn them. We must judge or evaluate everything around us to know what is right from wrong in our choices. However, we should not condemn others in our assessments even if their choices are not in accord with our beliefs. Discerning what's right for us and reacting without condemning others is difficult but also expected when we accept God's loving ways for our own.

Q: I see the difference between discerning and condemning, but are we bigoted because we choose not to befriend people who willingly make selfish choices? I feel it is a very different thing to avoid someone because of their race compared to avoiding someone who cheats on their spouse.

A: That, again, comes down to the intent behind our choice to avoid such people. Not every person of a different race wants to be your friend, so using discernment in trying to befriend others is wise. Going back to your example of avoiding one who cheats on their spouse, it is a very different thing to treat them as if "it had not happened" compared to condemning them. We can choose not to seek a closer friendship with some while still being friendly toward all and modeling our best behavior.

Q: So, to some extent, we're all bigots on the earth, although we may choose to be bigoted about different things. Is that correct?

A: It would be unfortunate if that is what you remember of this conversation. From a pessimistic perspective, your statement is truthful, but that is not how our Father sees anyone. The better way is the optimistic approach. Know that we are all unconditionally loved siblings who are just beginning to recognize our Father's love in everyone we meet. We may not do that perfectly yet, but with practice, we will persevere until we no longer think of anyone as "the least of these."

Q: So any form of bigotry is an illusion we believe is truth for as long as we ignore that we are all equally loved by God and of the same family. Using discernment to better react to the choices of others is correct as long as we don't condemn them for those choices in the process. Is that really the bottom line?

A: Essentially, yes. Most people have progressed to the point where they know it is better to say nothing aloud regarding their inner prejudices. Aligning our thoughts with being loving and patient will help us achieve the desired balance.

Q: Do you have closing comments that will help us understand and overcome bigotry?

A: The best time to overcome bigotry is "now." What better use of our time is there than doing all we can to become better people? You may find it helpful to identify some of the ways you feel you discriminate against others. Pick the one you'd like to improve first. As you work to see our Father's love, even in those you once discriminated against, the pattern to overcome any prejudice will become clear. Keep at it until all your choices align with God's loving ways.

My Own Significant Other

I was nearly 27 when I married Stephanie. It was to be my first and only marriage in this lifetime. Over the earlier years, I had relationships with a few long-term girlfriends and even lived with two of them. I went as far as to get engaged to one of them but called the marriage off. With Stephanie, it was different. We were engaged within three weeks of our first date and are even closer now than during the "romance period" of our early days together.

A long-time friend had watched me start and end several relationships over the years. Upon hearing I was madly in love and engaged so quickly, he asked, "Why Stephanie?" I found the question funny at the time, but only because I was so sure it was the right decision. As time went by, I became aware of why our relationship has improved rather than deteriorated with age.

We are a well-suited pair regarding important things like a sense of humor, intelligence, and especially our spiritual beliefs. We also complement each other with strengths in critical areas where the spouse needs support. Our shared love of dogs borders on worship, which seems to suit the two we have just fine. The question occasionally arises of whether we just got lucky or if there was a greater plan behind our union. I wondered about this myself, so I began seeking a metaphysical answer to this question.

I have investigated many psychics over the years. I've had some terrible advice from psychics, but such experiences were often funny and never a problem. There have also been a few psychics I found to be trustworthy. One in particular I trusted explained why Stephanie and I are such a good fit for each other. It seems that our coming together in this lifetime was far from accidental.

I was told that one of our marriage's great strengths came from the various relationships we shared in our past lives together. We had been married for many lifetimes. We had often been siblings or grew up together as cousins or in-laws. We were business partners and even soldiers together long ago.

In all those lifetimes, we learned to knock the rough edges off each other and to enjoy our time together. We had made a covenant before entering our current incarnations to marry and make a loving difference together using our symbiotic strength, drive, and dedication.

I do not know if our covenant made in the spirit plane is a rarity or if people always make such commitments. In comparing our respective childhoods and experiences, it was clear we had many opportunities to meet each other if we had not connected when we did. We lived within a few miles of each other. We shared an interest in the music programs of our respective schools. She worked as an instructor for my brother (he was a band director) for a time, and I was involved in a business that offered services to the local schools' music programs. That we would meet was inevitable. It seems our happy marriage was meant to be as well.

Because Stephanie and I have worked together so well in the past, we focus on improving our circumstances and environment rather than being distracted by finding fault or conflict with each other. I believe our shared worldview is what drew us together. We are blessed to be with each other and give back by sharing our love and enthusiasm with the people and projects we support. Having a great relationship comes easier when the couple's mutual goals are not selfish or reclusive but instead, support God's work in ways that bring us the greatest joy.

I offer this personal background and bias as an introduction to the chapter on relationships.

Relationships

Q: There are many types of relationships and challenges they bring to life. I want to start this discussion by asking about divorce. Why has the divorce rate risen so high in recent years?

A: This is a combination of many factors. We are on earth because we have forgotten to be loving, patient, and cooperative. Forgetting those qualities to become a better person is like playing chess and forgetting to move your queen or rooks. There is also a changing attitude in society today where we accept divorce as a reasonable resolution to our marriage conflicts rather than trying to work through our differences lovingly.

Q: And what caused that change in our attitudes?

A: The change was driven by outside forces and those from within. Souls incarnate into these vulnerable human bodies with a natural desire to ensure our survival. We bonded as families and communities, taking advantage of the respective strengths of all our members. As our communities grew and evolved, we depended less on bonding as families and more on sharing our strengths through technology. That evolution has resulted in higher divorce rates, fewer first-time marriages, less time staying with a given employer, and many other cultural changes when we feel more self-reliant.

Q: So you're saying we stay together mainly out of fear for our physical survival as humans? What happened to loving one another, serving each other, and having faith in God?

A: Love, faith, and service are great reasons to stay together, and an optimist would see life that way. Your first question about divorce focused on the pessimistic perspective of why we break apart rather than why we stay together. While these things are "two sides of the same coin," much can be learned by observing where each side of that coin, or approach to life, takes us in our thoughts.

Q: Is our desire to be self-reliant necessarily a bad thing?

A: Only when it leads to thoughts that separate us from the Whole. When we desire to be One with our Father while believing we can remain separate from those we dislike, we set ourselves up with an impossible task. A loving family cannot be divided against itself. Our greatest happiness can only be achieved by accepting that we are all One in spirit with our loving Father.

Q: What can you suggest as general guidelines to overcome conflicts between spouses?

A: Magnify your spouse's virtues while minimizing their faults. Do not expect perfection from your spouse, for they, too, are still discovering their greatness within. Build on your points of agreement while being patient and cooperative in overcoming your difficulties. Always think the best of your spouse, knowing that doing so brings out the best within them. And if things go poorly, do not easily lose faith or trust in either of you, for to do so supports a path away from your intended goal.

Q: You often speak of the importance of having a role model as the guide for doing something. Since Jesus did not "role model" the perfect marriage, who else can we look to for guidance?

A: So many famous couples of the past are known because of the tragedies that occurred rather than the role models they set. Romeo and Juliet, or Anthony and Cleopatra, are well-known but hardly the role models we should seek to follow. Look instead for the elderly couple who have been married for 50+ years and still hold hands when walking together. There will, of course, be aspects of their relationship that are not perfect. Still, you will also see how unconditional love conquers all and not condemning each other's faults actually brings them even closer together.

Q: Is there ever a time when divorce makes sense?

A: Of course, but not nearly as often as occurs. When one or both of the partners become addicted to drugs, alcohol, gambling, or sex outside of the marriage, these are all damaging to the relationship and difficult to overcome. Violence is especially addictive and quickly endangers family members. If it becomes apparent that the offending spouse does not have a strong desire to change for the better, then divorce can be the correct choice for all concerned. Seeking guidance from within through prayer and meditation as to when divorce might be the right choice is the better way to know with certainty.

Q: What causes some people to react with violence in a relationship when others, despite their differences, can work through a divorce peacefully?

A: We always attempt to resolve the challenges before us with the tools we have at hand. The more enmeshed we become in the earth, believing our entire existence is limited to the physical bodies, the more limited we become in the tools we can access.

First, we ignore our Father's advice so that loving, spiritual healing is no longer seen as an option. Next, we ignore the qualities of patience and cooperation that help us make better choices. What remains are only physical options to resolve our challenges. That often leads to conflict, coercion, and violence as seemingly the only remaining options to achieve our goals.

Q: So the more open and loving we are in meeting challenges, the more God can help us to see greater options. I understand how ignoring love, patience, and cooperation when resolving a conflict can make life difficult. What if the greater challenge comes in trusting others to measure up to the best within them? How do we trust others when there is a long history of reasons why we should not?

A: By not putting our trust in people so much as trusting our Father's loving essence within each of us. Humans will often not measure up, but our Father's loving ways will always prevail, and no real harm will come to us if we stand firm in our love, faith, and trust in Him.

Q: We will come to no real harm? How do you explain Jesus' trust in the Romans and Jewish leadership to do right by

Him and yet He ended up being crucified? You must admit that appears to counter the inevitable loving outcome you promised.

A: Jesus' crucifixion is probably the ultimate example in that regard. Though many would disagree, humankind has greatly improved since Jesus walked the earth. Our living conditions would not have improved had Jesus not measured up to the perfect Christ Consciousness within Him.

What if He had responded with hate and violence, taking full advantage of the unlimited power available to Him? Jesus could have easily overpowered His transgressors, but in so doing, He would have ruined everything He had sought to achieve in that same moment. Because Jesus only reacted with love, He resurrected a perfect and unharmed world, gaining the ideal role model of handling humanity at its worst.

Q: In other conversations, you have said that a perfect person will often make different choices than a less-than-perfect person in the same circumstances. That implies we cannot become perfect because we'll always fall short in our choices. Can you tie those concepts together so they don't seem at odds?

A: Even when our choices and actions are less-than-perfect, our attempts at becoming more loving are counted toward righteousness. From where most humans are now, expecting a perfect response is unlikely and unreasonable. We typically make progress a little at a time. Good parents know this and set their expectations accordingly, recognizing that we grow spiritually through our minor successes when we make loving choices.

In other words, to those who have attained Christ's Consciousness, we have the keys to His kingdom, and much is expected of us. If we still make selfish decisions, our access to our Father's knowledge, power, and abundance is adjusted accordingly. That is a new way of understanding the adage, "We are never given more than we can bear." It refers to wealth and power as much as fear and suffering.

Q: I understand it is not a good plan to allow everyone access to the power that could destroy the planet. While I'm certain Jesus could have "removed" the people who intended Him harm, He offered, "Father, forgive them, for they know not what they do." I'm pretty sure what He did would not have been my reaction if I had been in His position. Is God really okay with humans being less-than-perfect?

A: Yes. If you understand the unconditional love human parents have for their children, how much more does that apply when speaking of our Father? Everyone will eventually achieve the Christ Consciousness and look back on our earthly experiences as a time when we were having a "bad day." Jesus was not joking when He promised that we would all eventually do even greater things than He did.

Q: Looking at other types of relationships, it does seem that we often cut more slack to our family members than to our friends and acquaintances. Why is that?

A: It is a matter of perception and trust and part of the plan for being here. When we perceive someone as a family member, we often feel more obligated to them than others. This perception causes us to be more patient, forgiving, cooperative, and less condemning than we would typically be with those outside of our family.

Once we realize that every one of us is a divine sibling and beloved child of our Father, we will extend to each person the same loving consideration we do to our earthly family members. When we place our trust in others, we help them to trust us more in return. It doesn't take long for that positive cycle to build on itself.

Q: Does consistently giving the benefit of the doubt explain why couples (potential spouses) get along so well at the beginning of the relationship?

A: Indeed it does. We are often at our best on earth when we meet someone we're attracted to and want to spend more time with them. At the start of the relationship, there is no effort for us to be kind, forgiving, and playful. That wonderful romance period doesn't have to end, but it lasts only as long as we can magnify the virtues and minimize the other person's faults. This takes a turn in the other direction at some point in many relationships. Our old habits kick in, and we no longer react with loving kindness. That is the challenge for us all: keeping the love alive despite any transgressions that might throw us off.

Q: And how does a couple do that? How does it keep the love alive, as you said?

A: By remembering what it was like when things were going so well. It can help to write such feelings out from the start so that we can read and recapture our frame of mind if we start to slip. Knowing that we are each a beloved child of our Father means there is no question that each person is lovable. Our job is to measure up to the best within us, which always helps us draw the same out of others.

Q: How exactly do we draw the best out of other people?

A: It's hard to improve upon being the role model for the behavior we desire in others. If the other person is feeling down and depressed, asking them positive, helpful questions where the answers will put them on the right track works well. Encourage and compliment them too, especially in their talents that, when manifested, will make things better. Avoid condemning others even when we feel it is warranted. As said, always magnify their virtues and minimize their faults.

Q: But what do we do when our efforts are not returned? Sometimes, we can give, give, and it seems we don't get back the love and positive reinforcement we've offered.

A: It may seem that way, but such efforts are never wasted. Even if the person you offer love and encouragement to does not respond or return it, remember that we cannot give where we won't receive. Karma is often seen as a negative force in our lives because we mainly think of it when we are suffering. In truth, we can always expect to receive what we give, and that includes all the wonderful aspects of love and abundance as well as the consequences of selfishness.

Q: I agree that it is easy to forget that karma or "cause and effect" works to our joy and ensures we reap the selfishness we sow. Let me ask about our work relationships. What advice can you offer to make the best of them?

A: I can save a lot of time with the following advice. It doesn't matter what the relationship circumstances are, there is no difference in the attitude we should hold toward others. They can be family, friends, co-workers, members at your place of worship, or casual acquaintances, but a loving approach is always the way to go. The social rules of conduct may change according to our earthly interactions, but not in understanding that we are all One.

Q: I'm guessing a few military drill sergeants might disagree with that perspective. How can we expect to run a disciplined army with patience and brotherly love?

A: That really would be a challenge, but what makes an army necessary in the first place? When we come up against situations where a loving approach does not work, why that appears to be the case deserves consideration. Making our choices in accordance with a loving approach is always appropriate and keeps us on the right track. If everyone made loving choices, would we need the military?

Q: That's logical. Having a military is helpful only when fear and violence are tools we are willing to use in resolving conflict. Staying with the work scenario, how do you lovingly fire somebody?

A: First, do what you can to hire the right people; firing them is unnecessary. That is an option if they can be trained to do the job. If, after such efforts, it becomes clear they are not the right fit for the position, then how you explain that to them makes all the difference. It is true that when people are equally informed, they rarely disagree.

Q: Can you offer an example of how that might work?

A: You could start by reminding them of the steps taken to bring them up to speed or comply with what's required. Also, point out that you realize it has not been enjoyable for them to go through that process. Let them know what skills you admire in them. Let them know they will do well and be happier in a job that is better suited for them. In conclusion, staying where they are only works against their better interests because the right job awaits them elsewhere.

Q: They might easily take that as sarcasm, worsening the situation.

A: That could certainly happen, but much depends on how it is presented. If you have a history of being short, unkind, and sarcastic with this person, it would be better to use a less empathetic approach. But if you have always treated them with kindness and respect, then the chances are better that what you offer would be understood and accepted as the truth.

Q: The implication of what you just said is that how we handle ourselves prior to having to take any corrective action with a co-worker or employee makes a great deal of difference in how effective we can be in resolving such challenging issues.

A: Exactly. Too often, our past choices have already limited our current options for effectively resolving challenges. Our free will is always in charge, which applies to both people involved. Even if you resolve a conflict amicably, given the history between you, the other person may not.

Q: In closing, what words of help, hope, and encouragement can you offer regarding our having better relationships?

A: After all is said and done, how we get along together is the most important thing we do in life. If we take away all the "distractions" in our lives, what is left is our perfect Father and His beloved children. What should we do with our lives? Is survival worthwhile, seeking fame and fortune, or discovering all the secrets of the manifest universe? Those, indeed, are what I just referred to as "distractions." How we love, serve, and relate to each other is not often thought of as a soul's job description, but what else says it better than that?

With this concept's clarity, we can use it to create the desired changes in ourselves. Others may not always love and treat us kindly, but should we let that hold us back from living as Jesus showed us? Once we accept His loving ways for our own, we can find joy and see our Father in our relationships.

How Scary is Armageddon?

My wife and I spent a few weeks in the Holy Land and Egypt back in 1993. During that trip, we spent a few days floating down the Nile in a riverboat, stopping to take in the sights along the way. Our tour also allowed us to spend an hour meditating in the King's Chamber of the Great Pyramid in Cairo. We saw the shrine at Jesus' birthplace as well as two places claiming to be His tomb and site for His Resurrection.

We also visited the River Jordan, the Sea of Galilee, and the Dead Sea. The fortress known as Masada was imposing, and we visited Mount Carmel, where Mary and the Essenes were said to have lived. After we left Mount Carmel, our guide gathered us at the side of a mountain road. She told us that the vast plain before us was the fabled Armageddon, where the book of Revelation says a great war signaling the earth's final days will be fought.

On the other side of this great expanse was Jordan, but there were no people or buildings in sight from where we stood. It seemed like the vast area was waiting to fulfill its Biblical destiny. The silence of the tour group was ominous. Everyone felt the weight of actually gazing upon the place where our deepest fears might be realized.

I quietly turned within and asked if it were true that this place would eventually become the venue of the prophetic battle. The answer was, "It does not have to be." I understood that such prophesies are not set in stone. We always have the free will to make the changes we desire.

And with that in mind, the chapter on "War" follows.

War

Q: It has been said that more wars have been fought and people killed in the name of God than for any other reason. Is that true?

A: If you are asking if our Father sanctions this warlike behavior, then no, it is not true. If you are asking if humans believe "having God on our side" is an excellent justification for war, then the answer is yes.

Q: Is there ever a time when violence is the best answer to resolve a conflict?

A: I am not splitting hairs when I qualify the answer regarding which definition of "best" we are using here. Jesus would never choose to harm others. However, due to our past choices and limited perspective of our Father's loving ways, what is "best" for us is not always what Jesus would do but rather what Jesus would suggest we do. In many cases, people accept the wisdom of His loving ways only after seeing how useless violence is in resolving conflict. Nothing does that quite so well as experiencing war firsthand.

Q: But it is also said, "To the victor goes the spoils." If the conflict winner gets to take away the assets and humiliate the loser (or do worse), the side prefers violence. Doesn't that make "being right" a moot point?

A: You are correct in pointing out those are two very different things: prevailing through violence and being right. Resolving conflict through war determines the winner of the war, but not necessarily which side was right regarding the issues they fought over. The underlying conflict remains unresolved until all are satisfied that justice has prevailed.

Q: I think I understand what you're saying, but can you offer an example of what you mean?

A: World War I was fought over disputes that could have been resolved peacefully. Conditions worsened when the winners mistreated Germany by dividing their lands and resources. It took Hitler less than 20 years to pick up where

WWI left off because the German people strongly supported him to set things right.

The USSR took advantage of Germany's situation at WWII's end but couldn't sustain such an empire. No war was needed to dissolve the USSR's hold over those selfishly acquired lands. In much earlier times, provoking a war would have been the preferred solution of the USSR leadership to keep their empire together. They decided instead to let go peacefully. Humankind is getting better!

Q: I don't understand the idea of using war to keep a country together. What did you mean by that?

A: Having your country's existence threatened causes its citizens to pull together and withstand conditions they would not otherwise tolerate. The leadership knows if they win the war, then the confiscated wealth of the loser will help get their economy back on track. If they lose the war, the outcome will be no worse than the country destroying itself through riots and famine.

Q: But all of this sounds like a lesson in political science rather than a spiritual perspective of war. Where is God in all of this?

A: You make an excellent point. As long as we keep looking for political solutions that strive to maintain the status quo of the leaders in power, we are not looking to our Father for the right answers. We don't obtain lasting power and prosperity by taking it from others. We become powerful and prosperous by living lives of unconditional love. Who wouldn't want Jesus to lead them if they accept Him as the Christ incarnate? There is an excellent lesson in knowing that Jesus was much more effective in helping everyone on earth by pursuing neither a violent nor political solution.

Q: But if Jesus had been in political power, He would not have declared war. Isn't that half the battle…no pun intended?

A: Mohandas Gandhi's efforts to liberate India from Great Britain are a good example. Gandhi was able to help free India with a minimum of violence by effectively using organized civil disobedience. Jesus modeled the behavior, and Gandhi proved that it worked. Neither Jesus nor Gandhi held an elected political office. They both promoted a peaceful solution, and both of them succeeded.

Q: So what would happen if they had assumed political office to further their goal of peace?

A: They would not have been re-elected, for most citizens of both times favored violence over civil disobedience. For example, many preferred Peter's leadership to that of Jesus because he was a spiritual man who did not hesitate to take action.

Q: But can't more good be accomplished with greater control and political power?

A: As logical as that sounds, it is not true. There is a real difference in walking along the banks of a river heading in the same direction as the flow of water compared to being swept downstream in its current. Jesus and Gandhi needed to keep their feet solidly on the ground as they headed toward their goal. They offered help and encouragement to those swept along the river's currents to join them on the banks of truth. How effective could they have been if they had also been subject to the water's current (needing to be re-elected) instead of keeping their feet firmly planted in truth?

Q: So you're saying that while someone like Jesus would have remained perfect and unaffected by politics, He was more effective by not jumping into a rushing political river. In that way, He was better able to model an alternative way for each person to make changes in their own lives.

A: Correct. You mentioned how wonderful it would be to have Jesus as our political leader. Imagine how much better it would be to have all people share in the mind of Christ. Such a world would never fight a war and could only prosper.

Q: I understand that concept once it spreads globally, but what of those individuals today who abhor violence and still find themselves living in a country that declares war? What can be done then?

A: What your government chooses and what you do about it don't have to be in conflict, even in that case.

Q: I'm not sure how that would be if they drafted you into the military, yet you would refuse to fight.

A: There is no conflict in going through the training of how to be a soldier, though we object to actual violence. The citizens of a country should be willing to do their part to defend it. That is consistent with being "wise as serpents yet harmless as doves." However, it takes many non-fighting soldiers to support those who actively participate in the violence. If we do not spiritually gain from fighting, we will not be assigned a fighting role. However, if being in battle is part of reaping what we have sown or will otherwise help us grow spiritually, avoiding it only delays our progress.

Q: How can we be sure that works? Are you saying that any violence we encounter will help us to grow spiritually?

A: We will only "encounter violence" that is due to us karmically or because we agreed to put ourselves in harm's way in service to others. Jesus is a peaceful example of the latter. You are a good example of showing how this works karmicly. You joined the military right after Vietnam ended and retired just months before Iraq invaded Kuwait. You did this intuitively, knowing you were safe because it was not part of your greater spiritual path to serve in a war during this incarnation.

Q: But I was not serving in a capacity that would likely encounter combat. I guess from the number of "combat versus non-combat" jobs in the military, statistically speaking, most soldiers can rest assured of not having to fight.

A: Trusting in statistics more than God's loving ways is a personal choice I would not recommend. Such decisions are why humans seek political and economic solutions instead of a spiritual approach and trusting in our Father. Praying to Him to help us become better people and choosing a "solution" with less than a win/win outcome is why politics and spirituality rarely mix.

Q: What would have happened in WWII if the Allies had decided to cease all violence against Hitler? Wouldn't Hitler's imperialistic and genocidal ways have continued until he had taken over the world?

A: That's one way of looking at the immediate result. A non-violent approach requires patience and a forgiving attitude toward your violent transgressors. Civil disobedience, if organized well and done with a loving intention, is as powerful as any weapon on earth. Initially, however, it appears to be a dismal failure. The interesting part, although you would have to take this on faith, is that fewer people overall would have been hurt or killed had no shots been fired by the Allies in WWII. An approach of civil disobedience by the Allies could have been done so that Hitler would have eventually given up on world domination because it would have been seen as unproductive.

Q: But how much more suffering would the world have had to endure before Hitler's regime would have come to that realization?

A: In truth, much less was suffered due to the horrors of war. Humans have difficulty seeing things in this light because they focus on preserving their particular people, nation, and culture. The violence will stop once we regain the loving perspective that we are all One. Violent solutions no longer make political or economic sense when seen from a spiritual perspective.

Q: That sounds good, but it seems that day might be long in coming. Let's go back to some points you made earlier. It sounded as if you were saying that, on the one hand, we must protect our country, and on the other hand, we should do so without violence. That doesn't seem possible when the aggressors bring violence to our doorstep.

A: Looking at this personally is helpful because it is easier to follow. Applying what we know on a global level is the next step.

Secular law allows for the use of violence to protect our homes and family. So does spiritual law, but only if we can defend ourselves without adding greater selfishness to the conflict through hate, fear, and vengeance. Think of Jesus overturning the moneychangers' tables in the Temple. He could do that without negative feelings toward them, so He was spiritually justified in His aggressive actions.

Q: But since we can't react perfectly in love as Jesus did, isn't it better to avoid violence?

A: Yes. Remember that violence will not come our way if we do not need such experiences. It only comes to us when we have an opportunity to grow from working through it or willingly put ourselves in harm's way for the greater good of others. This is true for us personally as well as for all nations.

Q: Do you have additional words of encouragement to add in closing?

A: Only to reiterate the importance of seeking our Father's help resolving conflicts. Our immediate human reaction is to think we can "protect our interests" through violent means when provoked. First, we should understand that nothing can be taken from us that is truly ours. Second, peaceful possibilities for a win/win solution become more apparent as we seek our Father's loving help and guidance.

My Greatest Fear

I have always had an active and curious intellect. Even as a small child, I would ask questions well beyond my parents' ability to answer. I would ask how it was possible for the universe to go on forever or how time could continue without end. At six years of age, I asked, "If we live forever, what will keep us from becoming bored after we've already done everything a million times or more?"

My parents were impressed that I could think so profoundly, but I don't think they understood I was fearfully serious. Even at such a young age, I could work myself up into a near panic attack, thinking we were all doomed to an eventual existence of eternal boredom. Most of the time, I could distract myself from focusing on this, but it never really went away when I contemplated such things on my own.

I was in my 30s before I had an experience that removed any trace of this fear from my mind. I was alone in the living room, listening to classical music. I have a real love of the piece written by Edvard Grieg, "In The Hall of the Mountain King." It always moved my soul, and as it played, my mind raced through thoughts of how much joy the song gave me. My joyous reverie took a surprising turn that confronted my greatest fear.

I began to think that eternal boredom was not inevitable if I received such continuous joy, no matter how many times I heard this one song. I could see possibilities that I had not allowed my mind to consider before. I had often feared "contemplating the infinite" because it might start a panic attack. With this new perspective, I quickly realized that there are an unlimited number of universes with infinite souls so that we will never run out of new experiences to enjoy. I finally had an answer that showed me a way out of fear. But God took it one step further for me than that.

I sat there feeling elated that the fear that had plagued me all my life was finally resolved. But there was more to it than the logic of having infinite possibilities and people to entertain me. I clearly received this message: "The love of our

Father is so ultimately fulfilling that if all souls did nothing but bask in His presence for the rest of eternity, it would be enough." At that moment and forevermore, I knew this was true.

My new understanding that the unconditional love of God is never boring removed my greatest fear. If reading the Bible's book of Revelation makes you fearful, perhaps you'll remember this story as you read the next chapter.

Book of Revelation

Q: The book of Revelation is a source of great controversy. It reads like an end-of-the-world story that causes many believers to dread the days ahead. Is there any truth to the words we read in it?

A: If you are asking if things will occur like a red dragon sweeping one-third of the stars from the heavens and hurling them at the Earth, the answer is no. The Revelation was a vision given to the Apostle John in a meditational experience. Like the parables of Jesus, it is virtually 100% symbolic.

Q: Does that mean the vision was meant only for John? Does it have no meaning for the rest of us?

A: While it was intended for John, it has symbolic value for everyone on Earth. It was no error that it was included in the 66 books of the Christian Bible.

Q: Does John's vision describe the last days leading up to the world's end?

A: Not in the way that many believe it does. It is a symbolic story of the internal and external conflicts that occur when we choose to accept our Father's loving ways for our own. Once we succeed, we know the Earth is not our true home. So, in that sense, it foretells the end of our selfish attachment to this world, one soul at a time.

Q: You spoke of internal conflicts. What exactly does that mean concerning the Revelation?

A: In one sense, the body has constant battles inside. The immune system fights disease and impurities that can cause ill health. When hormones and histamines are secreted into the body's systems, opposite secretions make for the balancing. The secret to good health is to constantly balance our assimilations with our eliminations. Maintaining a perfect physical balance with a loving frame of mind would keep a body alive for any time desired.

Q: Balancing the assimilations with the eliminations means balancing what we take into the body with what is removed.

A: Correct. But this includes that which is taken and removed physically, mentally, and spiritually. Diet and exercise are important aspects of this balance, but so are prayer, meditation, and the loving intention of our thoughts and choices.

Q: So, do the internal conflicts you spoke of also occur when we are out of balance in our thoughts or actions?

A: Yes. The human body was chosen as the ideal form for the soul to experience and express itself in three dimensions. This is largely done through the endocrine system, which consists of seven different glands functioning as spiritual centers. Other animals have a similar system of glands, but none allow for the soul to integrate quite so well as the endocrine system does in Homo sapiens.

Q: What is the endocrine system?

A: You already know these seven glands as the spiritual chakras spoken of in Eastern philosophies. They are, in order, the gonads, cells of Leydig, adrenals, thymus, thyroid, pineal and pituitary glands.

Q: And what about those glands that make them more important than the brain or the heart?

A: They are not more important. It is a matter of different functions rather than importance. The soul fully expresses itself through these seven spiritual centers through the secretions and vibrations of each gland. As you are already aware, the body can continue after removing several of these glands, much the same as we still have limited function after removing a limb.

Q: And what exactly do these glands do?

A: There are the physical attributes for each gland, which medical science has already learned a great deal. There are also the mental manifestations of each. For instance, the gonads, medically speaking, have to do with reproduction and sexual expression. The gonads also represent the attribute of patience in balancing the carnal functions of the body with our spiritual purposes.

Q: Thinking back to the Revelation, the number seven repeats in many instances. Are those references in the Bible symbolic of the seven centers? If so, what would be an example of the symbol associated with the gonads?

A: The list of symbols you referred to is vast, but here are a few for the gonads. The color red, the first note of the musical scale (as in Doe, Re, Mi...), the calf, the root chakra, the church of Ephesus, the white horse, and even "our daily bread" as referred to in the Lord's Prayer.

Q: That's quite a list! So, the seven basic colors of the rainbow and the seven musical scale notes refer to the seven spiritual centers in our bodies?

A: You would find that statement humorous if you looked at it from a higher consciousness. The phrasing was much like the old belief that the sun and stars revolved around the Earth. A better way to word this is that our spiritual expression in human form manifests best in the number seven, so there are seven centers in the body.

Q: I'll have to take your word for that. So, does the number seven always represent the body's spiritual centers in John's vision?

A: Yes, but the different occurrences must be looked at in distinctive ways. The symbology of the seven seals, the seven angels with trumpets, and the seven stars all refer to a different understanding of the seven centers. Each changing manifestation of "seven" is given to identify a specific challenge we will encounter as we begin to make better choices.

Q: Can you offer an example of one of those interpretations?

A: Sure. No matter what we do here on Earth, there will always be spiritual, mental, and physical manifestations of our thoughts and actions. Every thought and choice results in our moving closer toward or away from the Holy Spirit, otherwise known as the Law of Love. When the carnal forces in the body are being spiritualized, as is referred to when "the lion lies down with the lamb," the physical conflicts described in Revelation represent the internal battles within the body.

Think of a time when you were scared, and adrenaline flooded your system. Moments later, you realized there was nothing to fear, but your body was heightened in readiness for danger. That is just one example of the ongoing battle between our hormones and histamines versus the mind controlling the body. When the body wins out over our better judgment, selfishness is often the result.

Q: I see and feel that one loud and clear. I never really thought of the adrenaline caused by fear as a chemical battle for dominance of the body. It seems ideally that the body's appetites would not influence our choices, but that is often not the case. Do I have that right?

A: Ideally, yes. The body ultimately takes its orders from the mind, but once a pattern is established, like an addiction, the body will come to expect that which it regularly receives. In psychological terms, the mind becomes codependent and enables the body's desires. Changing that pattern at the mental level does not immediately remove the physical addiction or habit we've developed in the body.

Q: Let me ask about the symbolism of some other images from the Revelation. Let's start with the four horsemen of the Apocalypse. What do these four symbols stand for?

A: An easier way to follow this is to understand a dividing line between heaven and Earth within the body regarding the seven spiritual centers. The four lower centers (the four horsemen) refer to the carnal forces, whereas the upper three centers are the more spiritual aspects of our physical being. The thyroid, pineal, and pituitary glands represent the Father, Son, and Holy Spirit of the Trinity, respectively. The four horsemen of the Revelation are the four lower centers, the gonads, cells of Leydig, adrenals, and thymus.

Q: Can you offer an example of the positive and negative aspects of the four lower centers?

A: As limited as this may be, how about all seven? The gonads represent the first separation from our Father, but this center can also symbolize perfected patience. The cells of Leydig represent living in fear at one extreme or a life of joyful enthusiasm at the other. The adrenals represent extremes of perfect faithfulness or faith so blind (following rules with no discernment) that it becomes a stumbling block. The thymus represents love or jealousy at its extremes. The thyroid is the will's center, used lovingly or selfishly. The pineal is the seat of the soul to remember and manifest all Truth…or not. The pituitary, at its best, is the master gland of the body, but we often remain lukewarm when applying its potential to guide us in His loving ways actively.

Q: You mentioned that chakras are a concept held by the Eastern philosophies. Would they all agree with the description you just offered?

A: Largely, yes. However, the order or sequence just given would be different for the last two glands, the pineal, and pituitary. Eastern philosophies have these in the reverse order, with the pineal being the highest.

Q: Why the discrepancy?

A: It has to do with the vertical positioning in the body versus the actual flow of spiritual energy. The Eastern philosophies prefer the former, whereas I offered the latter. It is more correct to think of these as being formed in the shape of the shepherd's crook, where the rising spiritual energy spills over into the pituitary after peaking in the pineal. In this way, our "cup runneth over," as given in the 23rd Psalm.

Q: You have now made reference to the Lord's Prayer and the 23rd Psalm, which has to do with the seven centers. Why is that?

A: Both prayers are meant to guide the spiritual energies raised through meditation in the correct order. The gonads respond to "daily bread." The cells of Leydig for "leading us away from temptation." The adrenals come next with forgiving our "debts and debtors." The thymus stands for "deliver us from evil." The thyroid goes with "Thy will be done." The pineal connects with "hallowed be thy name" and the pituitary with "who art in heaven."

Q: But the order of those key phrases in the Lord's Prayer is not in the sequence of their position in the body. Why is that?

A: Great question! The prayer first readies the top three centers and then cleans the lower centers for the spiritual energies within to rise to the top. It is much the same for the 23rd Psalm. Visualizing the movement of the energies as we say these prayers will greatly aid in attuning to the Divine.

Q: I'm guessing this same symbology applies to the main archetypal characters in the Revelation?

A: You "guessed" right. The symbols of the carnal forces, such as the false seer, the red dragon, and the beast, all make way for Christ Consciousness, which is symbolized by the lamb. The new heaven and Earth combine with these other symbols to represent various aspects of the human body and the mental and spiritual manifestations of the soul.

Q: I realize the details of this information would fill a book by itself, but I am curious about the numbers 12 and 24, given that they often repeat in Revelation. What do they stand for?

A: In truth, there are layers upon layers of symbology that exist throughout the Revelation that the finite mind may not fully understand. The quick answer to your question about 12 and 24 relates to the various systems in the body. The body can be divided into 12 systems: circulatory, lymphatic, immune, musculature, endocrine, etc. So the number 12 most often refers to the body as a whole as seen through these 12 systems. The number 24 is simply recognizing the potentially positive and negative aspects of each system which manifest in accordance with our free will.

Q: This is quite complicated, and I haven't started asking questions about the external conflicts you mentioned earlier. Would it be better to move on to that?

A: Yes. As you said, this subject is complex and not unlike discussing brain surgery without having the foundation to understand the answers. As you implied, it is a subject that is better left for other books.

Q: So what of the Apocalypse and the dire predictions of what lies ahead for the people of Earth?

A: It might be helpful to think of earthquakes when understanding the nature of the changes to come. The California area has earthquakes daily, albeit mostly very minor. On occasion, they have a major event, and the damage is only exceeded by the fear raised by the people who live there. The conflicts symbolized in the Revelation are no different. Changes to this planet and its people are inevitable, but will they come slowly, with many "small tremors" or perhaps from "massive quakes" causing much fear and damage as they relieve the pressure building from within?

Q: Having many small tremors to relieve the pressure is preferable to the devastation of a big quake, but do we have any control over that?

A: The people inhabiting the Earth have the most control over it. Our combined thoughts and attitudes cause fluctuations in how things change in this system. A good example is the shifting of the magnetic poles. Currently, the poles are moving at an average rate of around 40 miles per year. If the movement continues at that pace, the change will be so gradual that adapting to it will pose no major threat. However, in Earth's distant past, the poles shifted dramatically within a relatively short period, and the resulting global damage was devastating. Our collective thoughts and attitudes affect this rate of change. The more loving and patient we are as a people, the less threat there is from an impatient shift in our magnetic poles.

Q: Are you saying that the Earth has a consciousness that becomes impatient with us?

A: Not as you're thinking of it here. Our collective level of patience, or lack thereof, translates into the speed with which the poles will shift. Patience truly is the best measurement of our soul development on Earth.

Q: What about warfare and the other devastations the Revelation speaks of? Are major wars ahead for us with many earth changes as well?

A: The current trend is positive, meaning that great upheavals both on the Earth and politically are not inevitable in bringing things into balance. There will be tremors on both the political and geological fronts as things unfold at this time. However, the major devastation people often envision is far from inevitable.

Q: Now that's good news and quite comforting! I'm unsure how to phrase my next question regarding the tone of the Revelation.

A: You mean it sounds as if our Father is angry and impatient to seek His vengeance upon the Earth?

Q: Exactly, and that's always bothered me. The way I picture God in my mind when meditating compared to the pictures I get when reading the Revelation aren't even close. How can John's and my vision of God vastly differ?

A: A large part of the answer lies in how consistent I appear to be when speaking to you. The truth is always offered, but it is then filtered through the mindset of each individual. The Apostle John of that time felt that humankind had a debt to pay for all our suffering and selfishness. The worldview you held back in those times was not so different. Both you and the Apostle John have progressed to a more loving and gentle outlook over the past 2,000 years.

Q: But the Revelation is written to sound like God has something to prove to those who rejected Him. The ugly descriptions of "His vengeance" would be enough to alarm anyone. Did John interpret his vision back then to mean the future would unfold in a destructive and unscientific way?

A: Let me answer you with more than a simple yes or no. How is it received when you speak to others of the hope and joy you envision for the future?

Q: Sometimes well, but more often, others disagree, preferring a literal interpretation of what's described in the Revelation.

A: You can see that changes are slowly taking place as humans count time. The Apostle John lived in a time where far fewer people than now were on a gentle and loving path. It was quite common to think in terms of suffering and fear than to live a life of enthusiastic joy. The result of such thinking was that John's "filter" attracted a vision quite compelling to those who respond well to fear. If he had a vision today, it would be much kinder and gentler because of his improved understanding of our Father's love.

Q: So, the doom-and-gloom tone of the Revelation came from John's own mindset back then, which responded better to fear as a motivator?

A: Yes, but John's bias was not the only factor. As seen at that time, the future was more likely to bring major upheavals rather than simple tremors in achieving balance. The truth is that humankind is improving, and our world conditions have improved in many ways over 2,000 years ago.

Q: Now that makes sense. John's seeing the probable catastrophes of the future as it stood then, coupled with his own feeling that dire warnings are better motivators than gentle ones, answers why Revelation's picture of the future is so full of violence.

A: Yes, you have added your voice to so many others who know the future can be much brighter. The world is not approaching a cataclysmic end but rather a wonderful new beginning.

Q: Since you reminded me, what is the second coming of Jesus all about? Is He returning to Earth to do everything written about in the Revelation?

A: Jesus never left us, and His loving, peaceful message has not changed from when He walked the Earth. He is with us, always helping when we ask, and we will let Him. The one thing the Revelation conveys well, even as written, is the power of love. All power comes from love. When we are guided by love, our choices are already in balance. When we make selfish choices, we suffer as we learn the balance-seeking ways of the universe.

Q: The popular theories regarding the Millennium are either that Jesus returns as a full-grown human or that He comes back in a "glorified body," showing clearly who He is. Which is true?

A: Yes to both, and here's why. Have you noticed that no two people paint or draw Jesus in quite the same way? His return, as you call it, will be no different. Some will see Him as a man walking the Earth because they prefer to see Him that way. Others will recognize Him as the Christ incarnate and will see Him in the glorified form that best fits their expectations. Sadly enough, some will not see Him and deny Him again.

Q: How could someone encounter Jesus and not recognize Him?

A: You accept our conversations as being real enough. How many others would feel this discussion never happened? Communicating with the Divine is available to every person at every moment, but how many people make the attempt? Those who would not accept Him will not feel the need to go where He is. But if we have ears to hear, we will receive what we need most for our next steps on the path.

Q: Any last words of encouragement for us regarding all of this?

A: There is nothing to fear in the future. A happy resolution is assured, for our Father loves us all with an everlasting and unconditional love. Consider yourself lucky to be alive on Earth at this time, for you have the opportunity to make a difference in the course of humankind. With every temptation, our Father has provided a way of escape, and we should desire to make the path back Home easier for all. When we can read the book of Revelation with no fear in our hearts, we better understand its intended meaning. Let that mind be in you that is In Christ Jesus.

It Happened One Summer

I was 13 years old when my parents made arrangements for me to stay at a rural family camp in Virginia for an entire summer. The camp was sponsored by the Edgar Cayce organization, the A.R.E., or Association for Research and Enlightenment. It was quite a rugged place, with no hot showers or indoor plumbing, with the exception of the mess hall for preparing food.

The camp's concept was to learn a more loving way of life and apply that knowledge to how we treat each other at every moment. I was between the 8th and 9th grades that summer, and I had little practice in feeling loved and secure with my peers back home. It was a delightful change to have 100 or so people at the camp all getting along rather than looking for opportunities to make fun of each other.

Many remember this particular summer well. While there was little technology available in the camp, a small 12" black-and-white television was brought in on July 20, 1969. The TV was set up in the mess hall so everyone could watch Neil Armstrong take his first steps on the moon. Watching one of the greatest technological achievements in history against a backdrop of such a simple existence was ironic.

The changes I experienced personally that summer came subtly at first. For instance, I am not a vegetarian, but I chose to be one for that summer. The camp's diet was relatively healthy, even with the meat they served. I preferred to get two slices of the delicious homemade bread, which was offered as a perk for the vegetarians. At 7:00 AM each day, we gathered to exercise before breakfast, followed by a morning prayer and meditation. The water we drank came directly from an underground stream and was as pure and clean as possible. I adapted to this rural, loving lifestyle very quickly.

That summer, I stayed busy even without the usual distractions of a complex society. I spent time hiking the local fields and mountains. There were always daily classes in subjects like dreams, meditation, reincarnation, karma, and grace. Every class was given with an eye toward how the information could help us become better, more loving people. Even the sports we'd play were done with fun as the goal rather than establishing a winner of the competition.

In many ways, the evenings were the most fun for me. After dinner, we'd all sing songs around a big campfire. Some songs were spiritual, and some were more contemporary, but they were all chosen to be uplifting. The evenings always closed with meditation before we said our "good nights" and retired to our tents until morning.

If this sounds like a boring way to live, it is not. That perspective comes from a young teenager who was used to staying busy every moment with a lot of technology and very secular friends.

I had grown very fond of this way of life, and the months went by quickly. I stayed as long as possible, but soon, I had to fly back home to California or miss the first day of school. I had not realized how much of a culture shock that would be for me after having changed so much inside and out.

There were no barbers at the camp, so my hair had grown for the entire summer. In 1969, having longer hair was something only Hippies did, and I had indeed lived much like a Hippie in a commune for the past three months. I came home with a new, enthusiastic attitude toward life but found that the world around me had not changed.

I landed at LAX on a Sunday night, and the following morning, I started 9th grade at the same school I had attended for the past two years. People were astounded by the length of my hair, especially since I had kept it short all my life before that summer. The ridicule aimed at me by the other students was merciless, and that rough treatment continued from the faculty. I was sent home because my hair violated the school's dress code. That was not so bad because the teasing would not have stopped until I cut my hair.

I walked home thinking of how different life was for me now than it had been just the day before. I was thirsty and filled a glass with water from the tap in the kitchen. I took a deep drink and almost choked in the process. I had not realized how poor the water quality was in California compared to the mountain streams of Virginia. I stood at the sink, nearly gagging and feeling pretty sorry for myself.

Having already been called by the school, my mother found out about the rest of my day. I described the hazing I received from the other students and teachers and expressed how much I wished to return to the A.R.E. camp in Virginia, even if they didn't have hot showers or technology. Her response gave me a perspective that has stayed with me ever since.

She agreed how much better it was to live as I had in that rural A.R.E. camp where people only loved and supported each other. She acknowledged how shocking it was to abruptly return to the "real world" and remember how we typically treat our neighbors. She then placed the responsibility squarely on my shoulders, saying it was up to those who knew the difference to spread a loving worldview to the people who don't even think it is possible.

I had to grow up quickly in those few minutes to realize how right she was. I could choose to become a recluse and shy away from the world in hopes of avoiding the unkind words and actions of others. I could also show them that there is a better, more loving way to live where we don't pounce on each other for not conforming to the norm. While it would be many years before I began to understand the depth of such a choice, the seeds were planted and eventually took root in my mind.

You may find yourself reading about this uplifting worldview and doubting that we can all love and trust each other with patience and cooperation. I've felt such fear and doubt in my own life. I have also felt ultimate fulfillment from making a real difference in the life of someone who needed my help. Too many people know far more about fear and doubt than they do about love and joy. As Robert Frost said, taking the road less traveled makes all the difference.

Tangents

In many of the discussions that make up the Q&A chapters of this book, unrelated topics came up at times that were of interest but would not warrant an entire chapter on their own. Rather than leave them on the "editing room floor," they have been gathered here as a short collection of tangent ideas to the main chapters. This hopefully explains why these short dialogs sound as if they came from a discussion already in progress.

Technology

Q: It seems that improved technology has had quite an effect on our changing attitudes. Are all our technological improvements necessarily a negative trend regarding our spiritual development?

A: Technology by itself is a tool and only becomes a positive or negative factor in our lives as we choose to use it. For example, today's billionaires most often come from expanding the use of technological breakthroughs. Like any tool, technology allows us to do more with what we have.

Q: So, staying on the positive side of things, what are the spiritual advantages resulting from our improved technology regarding relationships?

A: It becomes much easier for people to connect with the help of technology. At one time, if two people weren't born in the same area, whatever karma they had between them would have to wait until they could be brought together. Having telephones to stay in touch, email, and internet dating services with faster, readily available transportation makes connecting and maintaining all kinds of relationships far easier than before.

Q: I can see that must be true, but how else is technology helping to offer greater opportunities for spiritual growth?

A: It is difficult to see now, but science is helping us better understand our relationship with our Father and all creation. While some believe science is actually "disproving the existence of God," eventually, people will come to know our

Father is the First Cause behind all creation and every new scientific discovery about it.

Q: Are you saying that science will eventually be able to prove the existence of God?

A: The connection or relationship of all things spiritual, mental, and physical is important to understand. Let me take a moment to explain the axiom, "The spirit is the life, the mind is the builder, and the physical is the result."

Our Father is pure consciousness, the only thing that truly exists. We can call that pure consciousness "spirit," with all energy, matter, space, and time as subsets or creations of His consciousness. When our Father's thoughts manifest, something akin to when we dream, they take on a quality of existence that consistently follows the rules or laws for how we souls can interact with each other in those realms. As we think of it on Earth, such dimensions are where creation flows freely without physical manifesEarthn. Like building a structure according to an architect's plans, we can choose to construct physical manifestations of our mental creations. So again, "The spirit is the life, the mind is the builder, and the physical is the result."

The connection science will eventually prove is that our Father's Consciousness first manifests as energy, as in "Let there be light." The creative process of our minds and desires cause energy/light to become waves/matter that vibrate and conform to our thoughts. The result of all matter conforming to our combined thoughts creates the physical universe within the space and time that we experience as humans.

It may help to think of our Father manifesting as steam, water, and ice corresponding to the spirit, mental, and physical realms. They are all from the same source or atomic structure yet manifest in three distinctive ways. It is no accident that Jesus often referred to water as a metaphor for life in understanding this concept.

Q: So science will eventually be able to prove the "relationship" between all matter, waves, and energy with God as the First Cause of it all?

A: Understanding this ultimate relationship of the body, mind, and soul as subsets of our Father opens many doors. While science will eventually be able to verify such a scientific relationship exists, the concept of our Father as the First Cause will be accepted by most humans long before the scientific proof is concrete. The days ahead are exciting times to be alive, and we should consider ourselves blessed to be on Earth now. Together, we are forging a fantastic future for us all.

Q: That is comforting to hear but not so apparent looking at the world today. What would be an example of technology's downside where it doesn't support us in becoming better people?

A: As I said, technology is a tool that allows us to do more with what we already have. That includes more selfishness and harm. Think nuclear weapons, for one, but don't forget internet scams and identity fraud. The impact of these selfish human creations has grown dramatically due to greater technology. As an example, the pornography industry has always been with us in some fashion, but because of the internet, it has come out of hiding and is now available in every home with a computer and internet access. When the selfish ways of humankind are constantly shared through videos and websites, it can present a biased perspective of the world, encouraging us to think we are all getting worse rather than better.

Q: I see your point, but can't the opposite also be true? If everyone made perfect choices, wouldn't our technology work for good by supporting a world view of peace and prosperity?

A: Well said! When we set our standards by the imperfections or "lowest common denominator" of the Earth, we push away the love, happiness, and perfection that our Father desires to share with us. Preferring a pessimistic view of life invites the question, "Just how miserable do we desire to be?" Building better relationships means making the best use of technology when it comes to cooperating with each other.

Pets and Animals

Q: I have often wondered how the animal kingdom fits in with our own spiritual development. How does this work?

A: The animal kingdom on the Earth conforms to our will and spiritual needs. Nature progresses according to our Father's loving ways without our presence and interference on Earth. Once we arrived on Earth, things changed to accommodate us.

Q: Can you give some specific examples of those changes?

A: Animals, in many ways, are akin to angels. They are part of our Father's creation and make only loving choices using the limited free will they were given. The only way such beings can act out of accord with the law of love is through the interference of souls (either by setting a poor example or deliberate training) who have the free will to make unloving choices. Just as the laws of physics can be used to harm others selfishly, this can also be done by manipulating the behavior of the animal kingdom.

A specific example of this would be when two dogs fight. When left to their own choices, once a conflict has been settled between two dogs, they most often part company without one killing the other. When humans take away their option of running away at the appropriate time, the dogs will continue to fight, often to the death. Purposefully breeding and training dogs to fight this way only adds to this ugly outcome.

Q: What about the positive side of animals?

A: Animals in the wild offer a beautiful example of how naturally the cycle of life works when we do not interfere with it. Nature always finds its balance without the help of humankind. Animals also offer an interesting perspective when it comes to self-preservation. When one life takes another, it is not done for selfish reasons.

Q: Then we should not have domesticated animals as pets. Is that the kind of interference you mean?

A: As with the rest of life, Nature has adapted to humans domesticating animals. And as our Father would have it, all things work to good for those who love Him. There are few better examples of unconditional love than what we receive from our pets.

This paraphrase of a well-known Bible verse describes the blessing we've been given through our pets: "Let this mind be in you that is always in Christ. When the Holy Spirit finds itself in the form of a dog, the role of a servant is accepted in love, and He becomes obedient unto death."

Memory and Recognition

Q: How do we recognize each other when we are not in physical bodies?

A: The vibratory pattern each soul emits is as distinctive an identifier of who we are as our voice and appearance are on Earth. In the spirit plane, each soul often chooses the image they wish to project. From an earthly perspective, that might resemble their physical body from a recent lifetime they shared with the person they encounter. The details of the age and state of health they project are also choices made to help in the recognition. The more acclimated a soul is to life in various spirit realms, the less such projections are needed to know one soul from another.

Q: If souls have always been and will always be, that means we already have an infinite amount of memories. How do we recall everything that ever has or will happen to us?

A: This is done by our natural access to what's known as the Akashic Records. A record of everything that takes place in eternity is recorded there, though such records would continue without a physical universe.

Q: Is there no privacy in the spirit planes? Is everything we've ever done so readily viewable by everyone without restriction?

A: You bring up a good point. There couldn't be better privacy assured for us than exists with the Akashic Records.

While everything is stored there, our access is limited according to our intention to seek information. If our intention is loving and helpful, then access is unimpeded. If we are just asking out of curiosity or even to hold the information against another soul, then we are not allowed access to such.

Q: So, how do we access the Akashic Records?

A: You might as well ask how we access our memories stored in the physical brain. It is as natural as that. A close approximation of the process in physical terms is that a resonant frequency connects our mind with the Akashic Records. The information sought is produced in accordance with the needs and intentions of the soul.

Q: It would seem that having an exact memory of all the selfish acts we commit would not be all that helpful. Are our memories edited to be helpful rather than painful when presented to us?

A: "Edited" is a good word to use in such a case. We can ask to access anything, but there is a "filtering process" to accommodate the circumstances you mentioned. We always have access to the lessons learned through our selfish choices when we are ready to review them, but then we will not feel the fear, guilt, and shame that once went along with the memories of those choices.

Employment

Q: What advice can be given to someone seeking a job?

A: There is little difference between the steps used to find the best employee and those used to find the best employer. Intuition, prayer, and meditation are the keys to succeeding in both.

Q: From the employer perspective, you previously mentioned that they should pray to attract the best employee to apply for the job. The employer would also pray to recognize the applicant as the answer to their prayers. How does this work the other way around?

A: The job seeker would pray to be led to apply for jobs where they would be a great fit for what is needed by the employer while fulfilling their own needs and desires in their work.

Q: But it seems so many employers manage through fear and intimidation. If an employee finds themselves in that situation, what can be done to improve it?

A: Karmicly speaking, this happens when one or both sides have something to learn from the experience. It doesn't matter which side or sides that applies to understanding how to proceed. The goal is to do what you know is right and love at all times without thinking that the other person must change. Setting a good example, even if you're on the receiving end as the employee, still works well to draw the best out of the supervisor or all of those in charge.

Q: If we know we cannot force them to change their ways, and indeed they don't, what then?

A: Then, as Jesus said, "shake the dust from your feet" and look for a better job that makes you happy while ensuring that the new employer receives everything they need from you as an employee.

Q: It seems unfair that a good employee must be the one to take the risk of changing jobs when the employer has the responsibility of being a good leader and steward.

A: Viewing such a move as a risk rather than our Father helping to improve one's situation is a matter of faith and perspective. If we approach a job search with fear and worry, we are innately attracting exactly the opposite kind of employer from what we say we desire. This is why people often attract the same tough challenges into their lives over and over, whether through their jobs or relationships.

Q: You're implying that the lesson is not tied up in the employer's behavior but rather that we must learn to have faith in God that all will work out well when we make loving win/win choices.

A: Yes, but it can be that both lessons have been presented simultaneously. By both lessons, I mean not trying to control or change others but having faith that our Father desires to provide a better situation for us in resolving every challenge.

Q: When you put it like that, it seems silly to not trust in God. What is the reason for such a fearful imbalance in our perspective?

A: Because we tend to think "business" is handled differently from spiritual matters. We have faith our Father will take care of us in eternity, but when it comes to living on Earth today, we somehow feel that our worldly needs are hardly worth His attention. This, of course, is not true. Our suffering most often is due to us karmically reaping what we have sown as well as receiving what we have fed with our thoughts.

Auras

Q: I am curious to know about the meaning and significance of auras. I'm defining an aura as the colorful energy field some say they can see around the human body. Do auras exist, and if so, what do they mean to us?

A: The aura acts like a scent to our noses or a feeling to our touch in identifying others. Whether or not we can consciously tune in and see another person's aura, we are still aware of it. When people speak of getting a "certain vibe" from another person, that feeling comes from our impressions gleaned from the auric pattern around them.

Q: Does the aura serve any purpose other than identification of who we are?

A: Actually, that is not the primary purpose of the aura any more than our human faces are meant as such. An aura is the energy field that is shared by the mental and physical bodies. From a three-dimensional perspective, it acts as a protector somewhat like the skin does for the body's inner workings. Infections can more easily attack the body where there are breaks in the skin. The same is true of the breaks we may develop in the auric pattern, albeit "infections" as seen on the mental plane are caused by negative vibrations rather than microbes.

Q: What does an aura look like to those who can see them?

A: You might liken them to a rainbow, although the colors displayed follow the vibrations given off by the person rather than the set colors in refracted light. One might also be able to see symbols in the auric pattern. Both the auric colors and symbols can be read like a resume of the person in understanding who they are.

Q: How often does a person's aura change?

A: In truth, our auras change with every new thought. The spiritual attunement of the person observing an aura often doesn't keep pace with such nuances. In such cases, the auric pattern may appear more static, like a snapshot, and only change each time they make a renewed effort to observe the changes.

Q: How can "breaks" in the auric pattern be healed?

A: These are caused by an imbalance in our thinking, particularly with addictions. A break often occurs at the location of the spiritual chakra or center when we are out of balance. Physical ailments may also be reflected as breaks in the corresponding area of the aura. As with most illnesses, prayer and meditation work well to heal these breaks. For permanent healing, however, the imbalance in our thinking must be aligned with love rather than the selfishness that caused the break to begin with.

Astrology and the other "ologies"

Q: Many people are believers in astrology. What value is there in studying the movement of planets and stars?

A: A great deal if done correctly. The specific conditions that surround each body on the Earth are reflected in the ongoing celestial movements. A study of astrology will allow anyone to generally predict major shifts in the life conditions for each soul incarnate.

Q: That sounds like predestination already has set in place what will happen. Is that correct?

A: No. There is nothing stronger in all creation than our free will. However, from an earthly perspective, our past choices result in the future conditions we will karmically encounter. Remember that the mind is the builder, and the physical is the result. From that perspective, what happens to us in the physical is actually a past condition of everything already set in motion by our thoughts and choices.

Q: So even if something is "written in the stars," so to speak, can our free will still dictate what will occur?

A: Yes, but not quite as you're thinking of it. Our free will is the strongest factor in the karma equation, but don't forget that our free will has already set our life's conditions in motion. When we karmically encounter the results of our past choices in the present, this is not pre-destiny but reaping what we have sown. The longer we procrastinate in changing our selfish behavior, the fewer options we will have to change the future.

Q: Is that like dropping a glass and not making an effort to catch it until it has almost hit the ground?

A: It does work in a similar way. If we wait too long to react, though the glass has not yet hit the ground, we don't have reflexes fast enough to catch it in time.

Q: I am somewhat familiar with numerology. As with astrology, is there any value in the study of numbers in relation to our lives?

A: Yes, but the depth of numerology goes far beyond what most earthly experts in the field realize.

Q: What do you mean by "far beyond?" Can you give me an example?

A: You are aware that different spectrums of light can yield an entirely different way to visually see the world around us. For instance, what we can't see with normal human vision might suddenly come alive if we can see infrared heat signatures. If we were able to see broadcast waves and decipher them, we would not need a TV to tune into the programs that constantly surround us in waveform. In a similar way, it is also possible to see the world around us using a filter or tuning device responding to numbers.

Q: What would that look like exactly, seeing the world around us from a "numbers" point of view?

A: A recent movie called The Matrix offered a reasonable visual example of this. A video monitor showed an alternate reality (the virtual Matrix) as numbers flowed along in columns streaming from top to bottom. Now imagine seeing those numbers all around you, but they are arranged so they outline three-dimensional shapes rather than columns of numbers on a flat two-dimensional screen. While that bears little resemblance to a true numerological view of the world, it is a fair description when answering your question in three-dimensional terms.

Q: That explanation sounded like a nice way of hinting I should move along to more relevant questions.

A: That would be wise and far less bewildering for most.

Q: Perhaps I can save some time and include all the other "ologies" in one question. There is phrenology, iridology, palmistry, reflexology, and many more. Is it reasonable to ask a blanket question regarding their validity?

A: Yes, since they all have a place in helping us understand, prepare, and respond in love to the conditions around us.

Q: I don't know a better way to ask this than to wonder why there are so many methods of discernment for us to use.

A: Your wonderment implies that these methods were planned ways to discern the secrets of the body and upcoming conditions. The truth is that everything in the universe is naturally connected, so the "ologies" can't help but display that which has already occurred and that which will come if we know how to read the signs.

Q: I assume that includes things like tarot cards, I-Ching, and other methods that are not related to the body?

A: Yes. As with any of these methods, the information available is limited only by the ability of the person offering the reading.

Q: Does it follow that the better a person is at tuning in to such information, the greater their spiritual development?

A: It can be, but that is not always the case. Psychic abilities are able to be strengthened just like a muscle in the body. In the same way that we wouldn't assume to guess the spiritual development of a muscle-bound man coming from the gym, neither is having strong psychic abilities the best measure of our spiritual development.

Q: And what would be the best measurement of our spiritual development?

A: Patience. Demonstrating great patience in all situations can only come through a better connection with the divine within. Look to those souls who show patience with others, especially themselves, and you can't help but see the relationship.

Two Visits From My Dad

My earthly father passed away in January 1982. He was not quite 65 years old, but he had health challenges for most of his life. Still, it was quite a shock when I received the news that he had died in his sleep at home.

I rushed over to be with my mother. My wife met me there (we were still engaged at that point) along with my brother, Bill. Stephanie and I had only been together for eight months when my father passed away. She was already familiar with the family's spiritual beliefs and shared our certainty in a God of unconditional love. She told me later that the loving and peaceful way my family handled the passing of my father was the greatest proof she had witnessed of how convinced we were of our beliefs.

A week later, Stephanie and I visited my mother and sat on the couch in her living room. My mother was finishing up in the kitchen, and we were speaking loud enough to be heard from the other room as she put the dishes away. We were discussing whether Sigmund (my parents' sheltie dog) was able to see my father even if we were not. We all agreed he probably could, but he would not react strangely because it would seem normal to him.

We were silent for a moment, and then a curious thing happened. The stand-alone console TV in the living room served as the resting place for a lamp, a figurine, and a few dog toys. No one had touched any of the objects on the TV since my father had died the week before. Suddenly, in that moment of silence, the rubber ball we would throw for Sigmund started moving on its own. It rolled off the end of the TV and bounced on the living room floor.

Stephanie and I were stunned as we watched this happen. We had no sooner been asking if Sigmund could likely see my father after his death when this event with the ball occurred. No breeze, earthquake, or any earthly force caused that ball to move after sitting still for a week or more. My mother entered the living room, and we described what had happened. She just smiled. To do more would invite a flood of distracting emotions, and so we all enjoyed the moment together in silence.

Many years later, I was working with a spiritual group whose purpose was to practice inspirational writing. I used the same technique in writing most of this book: meditating and listening to the guidance we received for the questions we asked. My father had been gone for over 20 years by this time, so when we all agreed to meditate and see if we could contact someone who had died, my mind was on relatives who had passed much more recently than he.

As I sat in the stillness, I was amazed as a thought burst into my mind. It was as if someone was talking to me, but there was no audible source for the words I was mentally "hearing." The opening words were, "Hey, Butch!" That was a term of endearment that my father used for both my brother and me. We were both born in Texas, but we grew up in California. I had rarely heard anyone use the nickname "Butch" except my father for the two of us.

I was able to have a conversation with him, although it didn't last long. My father told me he was doing well, that he loved us all, and that he had not reincarnated, as yet, into another human body. I asked about his mother and brother, who had died since he had passed from the earth. He laughingly confirmed they were over there and doing fine. I asked what was so funny, and he mentioned how unhappy they were. Without using words, he conveyed telepathically what he meant.

My grandmother and uncle had both been Southern Baptists. They were certain that they were saved by believing in the blood sacrifice of Jesus and that they would be entering into heaven after the Last Judgment. They were unhappy to find that was not how it all worked. Learning that living many more human lifetimes on earth was the best path into "heaven" was not what they wanted to hear. Their expectation of "instant perfection upon death" met up with the reality that "God never interferes with our free will." So we must freely choose His loving ways for our own rather than having God interfere and cause us to make choices as He would.

Others have told me of my father contacting them after he died, but that was the only conversation I personally had with him…so far. I was blessed to have it, short as it was. It served to confirm for me even more that death does not part us.

Death

Q: Death is not a popular subject, but one we humans all eventually must face. Is there an encouraging perspective you can offer to start this discussion?

A: While we can use the term "death" to describe the end of the life of a physical body, a better term to use would be "transition." Life is eternal, and there is no death; it is only a transition of consciousness from one realm to another.

Q: And where are these other realms we go to when we die?

A: In truth, there is no relocation of consciousness. Think of our transition upon the death of the physical as changing the channel on a television. As we change channels from one program to another, did we physically relocate to those "other realms," or is it better described as shifting our focus and tuning into a different reality?

Q: That example is easy to understand, but why can't we see the souls of the people who transitioned after their physical bodies died?

A: That's similar to asking how to keep the channels separated on our television tuner. Each channel is vibrating at a different rate. There are physical laws that maintain the separation between these other realms.

Q: Aren't there people who can access or see more than the earthly realm? How are they able to do that?

A: Think of having more than one television in the room where such people can see a different channel on each screen. It is up to them to choose a particular program for their focus, or they can try to take in more than one program at a time.

Q: Is that how mediums channel departed souls from the "other side?"

A: A medium is a person who allows souls from the other side to communicate temporarily with someone still in physical form. Some can consciously listen to both sides without giving up control of their body. Though it was often done humorously in the movie Ghost, the channeling and listening methods of spirit plane communication were acted out.

Q: People seem to share a consistent experience of seeing a tunnel with a white light at the end when having a near-death experience. Why do so many share this "tunnel" experience?

A: It is the lowest common denominator of the transitioning experience. The tunnel the soul sees upon transitioning consists of the endless realms of existence. The white light at the end of that tunnel acts as a beacon to guide us to where we should go next in our spiritual development. As a soul acclimates to its new surroundings, the tunnel is seen as the connecting pathway between the dimensions or realms. While it is ultimately our Father, the white light is more of a compilation of all the souls, angels, and universal laws helping to guide us to where we should go next.

Q: Then the tunnel is like a long hallway with many doors leading to these different realms?

A: In three dimensions, that is a reasonable way to explain this concept. Depending on their spiritual development, many of those "doors" will not open to the soul. Access to a greater number of "doors" comes in accordance with our acceptance of the loving ways of our Father.

Q: You make that sound like an exclusive club designed to keep out the riff-raff.

A: Some may see it that way, but it is incorrect. All are welcome, and no doors are denied to us when we are ready to enter. It might be better to consider admission to some realms of great love and light as requiring a certain dress code. Think of that dress code as the measure of our willingness to treat each other lovingly and choose as Jesus would. The more loving we are, the fewer restrictions there are to the doors we may open.

Q: Beautifully said! I understand the difference in how we view such restrictions. While we can feel that others hold us back, the truth is that our freedom is only limited by the selfish choices we make. What about the white light? How should we think of that?

A: In the near-death experiences you've read about, it is how the conscious mind often perceives the various aspects of the ever-abiding presence of our loving Father. That is to say that the experience of being drawn toward the white light upon transitioning is felt rather than seen. When people remember a near-death experience, their human mind translates those feelings into a description we can understand with the five senses.

Q: Other than the "white light in the tunnel" experience, what else happens when the human body dies?

A: Too many variations occur to try to detail them here. Generally speaking, we first acclimate to our new surroundings as we go through what is best called a Life Review. That is where we can review the human life just passed from the standpoint of truth rather than a biased view of any other perspective.

Q: So we see everything we did in the life just passed as God sees it rather than how we remember it from our biased perspective?

A: Correct. At first, the Life Review is like a dream, with our memories of the life just passed playing before us like a movie. As the mind acclimates to the spirit realm, our life's memories become crystal clear in the lessons they present. Self creates any feelings of condemnation felt by the soul during the Life Review. The Life Review is only meant to be instructive and helpful. However, it is almost inevitable that we feel fear, guilt, and shame for not having measured up in that life as we had originally planned.

Q: I'm not sure I understand that fully. If no one is condemning us, why do we feel so bad?

A: We may feel remorse over things we have done, but more often we see and finally understand the tremendous opportunities we simply passed up. Our "sins of omission" often bother us in the Life Review more than the selfishness we acted upon.

Q: If there is only a constructive review of the life just passed without condemnation by others, why are so many afraid of death?

A: Our dread of the unknown is our biggest fear, but right on its heels is our inner knowing that we will have to face our sins and acknowledge all the missed opportunities that were set before us. Those combined conditions account for most of the misunderstood anxiety humans experience when contemplating death.

Q: Will we ever get to the point where death does not bring such fear?

A: Yes. The time will come when death will be seen as a simple transition. We will exit the Earth and go to other realms when we choose rather than wait until our bodies can no longer continue.

Q: Could you say that again using different words?

A: The human body does not have to die. If we balance our assimilations with our eliminations (everything we take into the body with everything exiting it), the body can continue for as long as desired. When souls first entered into three dimensions, they entered and left as they desired rather than through the birth canal and death of the body. It will be this way again once we raise our consciousness sufficiently. The common term for this intentional transition is "translation," or to translate from one realm to another.

Q: That sounds like what happened with the Resurrection and Ascension of Jesus.

A: Exactly right. The role model Jesus provided for all, not just in life but also in death.

Q: It occurs to me that perhaps being born into a human body is seen as dying from the "other side." Is that accurate?

A: As logical as that seems, it is not the same. The reason is that from the other side, it is understood that life is eternal. That we live as humans for a period of time to help in our spiritual growth is not a theory or religion, but an absolute fact. Depending on our level of awareness, we foresee the conditions and challenges we will encounter in the future, and we even make choices regarding what lessons we'll take on and which we'll tackle in another lifetime.

Q: So, does our greater understanding of the entire process remove the fear of making the transition from spirit to the physical?

A: There is still the sadness in the parting. However, souls can still communicate directly when the human body sleeps. On the other hand, our certainty that life is eternal makes incarnating in human form more like taking a business trip rather than fearing we may part with loved ones forever. That makes all the difference in why death is not seen in the same way from the two perspectives.

Q: Adding to all the "unknowns" for those in three dimensions are the theological possibilities of heaven, hell, or even oblivion. Such religious beliefs hardly comfort humankind's fear of death, no matter how much faith we have in a loving God.

A: Correct, but such fears are short-lived after transitioning to spirit. A typical reaction from one who believes that accepting Jesus as their savior absolves them of their sins is "disappointment." They eventually realize that it is up to us to freely accept and follow His loving ways rather than being transformed into perfect souls. After a whole human lifetime of believing they would attain heaven after they died, the disappointment is understandable.

Q: It sounds like we get over it, but how much time does that usually require?

A: Many other dimensions have their versions of time, but most do not measure it as we do here. So, the question of how long it takes to get back on track after being "disappointed" does not translate into days, months, or years. Suffice it to say it does not take long for most.

Q: I'll take your word on that one. However, a question arises as to whether we all share a common spiritual perspective or even a common religion after we are released from human form.

A: Great question! The answer is no. There is greater agreement regarding the existence of our Father, but that does not mean that all agree on how we live and treat others.

Q: I'm having trouble understanding what kind of a disagreement there can be if we all agree that a loving God exists and we should all follow the Great Commandment and the Golden Rule. Can you give me an example?

A: Think of a conversation between General Patton and Mother Theresa. Both have always believed in our Father as the First Cause and Creator of all. However, ask them to suggest how to organize and encourage people so that they may achieve their highest potential, and you will find two varying opinions. Add a third person to the conversation, and you've added yet another opinion, and so on.

Q: It sounds like you're saying that a loving approach does not have to be all "kittens and rainbows" when it comes to treating our neighbors.

A: Correct. Some very loving souls prefer a disciplined life. We may all agree that love is the answer, but some prefer to live according to a precise schedule and rules. They feel we would all be better off if everyone held to such standards.

Q: It's interesting to think that there could be a difference of opinion on such an important spiritual point when the souls have developed beyond what can be learned on Earth.

A: That is not to say that the souls who prefer stricter standards are not loving. They believe that suffering brings greater understanding; for some, it does.

Q: What happens to a soul who lived on Earth as a confirmed Baptist or Muslim? Is it harder on those whose religions followed strict rules once they find there is no Last Judgment?

A: Part of the adjustment process is remembering who we are and why we chose to incarnate on the Earth. When a Baptist passes over, they remain a "dead Baptist" for a while until they acclimate and begin to remember their life in spirit before their human life. It's like recovering from amnesia, but most do so before the Life Review is finished.

Q: What is it like for a baby who dies? Do they have trouble adjusting, having never been fully acclimated to the Earth?

A: It is no different for a soul who dies as a baby. They remember who they are and their experiences before incarnating as a baby. Those past memories help to build a foundation to get back on track, so to speak.

Q: What about earthbound souls who don't let go of three dimensions when they die to move on to the next steps on their spiritual path?

A: Other souls and angels are specifically assigned to help them remember who they are. It is much easier for all of us to ignore such help when in physical form. However, some show an amazing ability to continue to ignore such help even after physical death when we no longer have a conscious mind to hide behind.

Q: Does the conscious mind help us hide? What does that mean exactly?

A: Think of sitting in a living room with others and wanting to shut them out. The conscious mind can be used like a television and volume control to override those in the room with us. The more they try to get our attention, the louder we turn up the volume on the television.

Q: How do people ignore others when they have passed over and have no conscious mind to run interference?

A: Have you ever watched someone so intent on one thing in the room that nothing else matters? We have all become experts at blocking out what we'd rather ignore. The human body offers many diversions in the form of distractions, ailments, and disabilities, which we often use to hide from the things we'd rather not think about.

Q: Can we develop any physical infirmities when not in human form?

A: Not as you are thinking of them, no. Many souls feel the need to sleep regularly after passing over because they have become used to that cycle on Earth. We soon learn that sleep is unnecessary, but we can still put our minds on hold and rest, even without a physical body.

Q: And what about mental illness? Do mental illnesses go away after we pass over?

A: Those illnesses caused by a challenge with the physical brain cease immediately upon the body's death. If the mental illness was formed from a fearful event or trauma, we carry it with us in the same way as the rest of our choices and experiences affect our thinking.

Q: Can more be given regarding an experiential perspective when we die?

A: The initial experience is much like we perceive a dream. We start as passive viewers with a vague awareness of what is happening around us. Gradually, we become more aware of our surroundings as we begin to understand that we're not dreaming. This is typically when the Life Review takes place.

Eventually, we come to enjoy our newfound freedom of movement and lack of other limitations found in the physical realm. In short, our lifetimes on the Earth will be seen as "lesser experiences" when compared to our infinite other encounters yet to come.

We then prepare for our next incarnation on Earth in education and planning for the life that will be of the greatest help and hope in our spiritual path.

Q: In closing, what encouragement can you offer on death?

A: We will all come to see that death does not part us from anything. While it is a natural process of the earth experience, death is not natural to the eternal soul. To be afraid of death is something like a prisoner being afraid of the day he will be set free. Fearful situations like that do occur on Earth, but they do not happen once the individual is truly rehabilitated. After we learn to live our lives as Jesus taught, we will no longer experience death. Never doubt that day is coming!

A Message For You

Q: The readers of this book have observed as we have gone back and forth over the subjects of each chapter. What is shared here is not just for me. I want to help the reader feel included in this message of love and encouragement, knowing it applies directly to each of us. In closing this book, can a message be given directly to those who took the time to read all we've discussed?

A: The reader should take in the following words, knowing they are given to connect with each individual. This is not misleading because every soul is the beloved child of our Father:

You are to be commended. So few of us on earth persevere in becoming better people. You have come seeking, and as a result, much has been given to help your spiritual development. What will you do with such knowledge?

First, you should never forget what a delight you are to your Father. Seeing our lives unfold on the earth often does not catch us at our best. But never forget that we were created to be companions and co-creators with Him. Perfection has been ingrained within us, and Jesus showed us perfection is possible if we follow His example. You have already awakened that pattern through your desire to improve. As you use what has been given, more will be added.

It is time to recognize the greatness within all His children. We already see it within some, but the next step is to recognize it in everyone and encourage them to be their best. To be sure, excluding even one soul from our divine family leads us down a dark path that cannot succeed.

When we begin to see that even the vilest act of humankind is just the unconditional love of our Father misapplied, we learn how to treat even "the least of these" with the same love and respect as the Master. We must always be "wise as serpents, yet harmless as doves" in protecting ourselves and loved ones from harm, but we can do so without fear by continually pursuing the best outcome for all concerned.

Nothing you can do will keep your Father from loving you. Believe it! After you become convinced of this, your fear, guilt, and shame will no longer keep you apart from the Whole. You cannot fail in making your Father happy, for He remembers the great beauty you have already added to His creation, and He already sees the joyous times ahead once you again accept Jesus' loving ways for your own.

You were promised to do even greater things than Jesus showed us. That is what lies ahead for you as you move toward the goal of becoming all you can be. Know that our Father has already prepared a way of escape with every temptation. The only question remaining is, "How long can we resist the unconditional love of our Father?" The time is now, and the way is clear. Let this book be your catalyst for the changes you desire to make. So be it!

Made in the USA
Middletown, DE
01 August 2025